Tony Davis once own
collapse around him
Fiats, Alfa Romeos, Jaguars and Rovers. Who better to write a paean to slapdash, a tribute to shoddiness and an ode to joylessness and mediocrity?

Extra LEMON!

More heroic failures of motoring
TONY DAVIS

BANTAM
SYDNEY • AUCKLAND • TORONTO • NEW YORK • LONDON

Photographic credits: while every effort has been made to contact copyright holders, the publishers will be glad to make good in future editions any errors or omissions brought to their attention.

EXTRA LEMON!
A BANTAM BOOK

First published in Australia and New Zealand in 2005 by Bantam

Copyright © Tony Davis, 2005

All rights reserved. No part of this publication may be reproduced, stored in a retrieval system, transmitted in any form or by any means, electronic, mechanical, photocopying, recording or otherwise, without the prior written permission of the publisher.

National Library of Australia
Cataloguing-in-Publication Entry

Davis, Tony.
Extra lemon.
ISBN 1 86325 550 8
1. Automobiles – Humour. I. Title
629.2220207

Transworld Publishers,
a division of Random House Australia Pty Ltd
20 Alfred Street, Milsons Point, NSW 2061
http://www.randomhouse.com.au

Random House New Zealand Limited
18 Poland Road, Glenfield, Auckland

Transworld Publishers,
a division of The Random House Group Ltd
61-63 Uxbridge Road, Ealing, London W5 5SA

Random House Inc
1745 Broadway, New York, New York 10036

Extra Lemon! is partly based on 'The Mightabeens', a series conceived and written by the author and first published in *The Sydney Morning Herald*; and the 'Lost Cause of the Month' section in the author's 'On the Verge' column, which appeared in *Motor* magazine.

Acknowledgments
The author didn't thank anyone with the previous book, largely because he thought no-one would want a dedication in a book named *Lemon!* However, Carolyn Walsh, Pedr Davis, Jude McGee, Jessica Dettmann, Tim Vaughan, Claude Ludi, Joshua Dowling, Alistair Kennedy, Mike Toten, Andy Auchterlonie, Fred Diwell, Stephen Knox, Michael Browning and Phil Scott all deserve generous portions of praise and thanks, and one day the author will find the right forum in which to give it to them.

Internal photographs supplied by Marque Publishing Company, PO Box 1896, Gosford NSW 2250
Cover photograph by Peter Bateman. Lightburn Zeta Sports kindly loaned by Fred Diwell
Cover and Internal design by Darian Causby/www.highway51.com.au
Printed and bound by Griffin Press, Netley, South Australia

10 9 8 7 6 5 4 3 2 1

Contents

Introduction • ix

Jaguar XJ220 • 1
Prenvic • 4
Nissan Cedric • 5
Chevrolet Corvair • 6
Lightburn Zeta Sports • 10
Fiat Croma • 14
Quasar • 17
Austin X6 • 18
Bond Bug • 21
Ford Cortina Six • 22
Fiat ESV 1500 • 25
Subaru 360 • 26
Datsun 280ZX • 30
Lada 110 • 33
Hillman Imp • 34

Toyota Corona 'Starfire' • 38
Moller Skycar • 41
Honda Z • 42
Zil • 45
Holden Piazza • 46
Scamp • 49
Oldsmobile Toronado • 50
Ford Falcon EA • 54
Ligier • 57
VW Country Buggy • 58
Jensen Interceptor • 62
Leyland Force 7 • 65
Chrysler Centura • 66
Triumph Mayflower • 69
Holden Camira • 70
AMC Pacer • 73
Purvis Eureka • 74
Panther Rio • 77
Ford Landau • 78
Panther 6 • 82
Ssangyong Korando • 85
Suzuki X90 • 86
Sabra Sports • 89
Tucker 48 • 90
Ford Gyron • 95

Ilinga AF2 • 96
Daihatsu Bee • 99
Holden Brougham • 100
Moskvich • 103
Toyota 2000GT • 104
Ford Pinto • 108
Nash Metropolitan • 112
Valiant CM • 116
Toyota T-18 • 119
Daimler SP250 • 120
Haflinger 700 AP • 124
Edith • 127
Austin Freeway • 128
AMC Gremlin • 131
Tatra Electronic • 132
Holden HD • 136
Standard Vanguard • 139
Bristol Blenheim • 140
Alfa Romeo Montreal • 144
Amphicar • 147
Isuzu Minx PH10 • 148
Trabant P601 • 152
Ford Falcon XK • 156
Toyota Publica 700 • 159
Davis • 160

Introduction

The dull, the bad and the ugly

Today's high-tech wonder-car can be the latest and greatest only for a fleeting moment. Someone will always come along with something faster, sleeker or more sophisticated.

A lemon, however, can stand out forever.

This lasting quality is not the only thing that makes the clangers of the automotive world far more interesting than the successes. People find it hard to become emotional about the commendable achievements of cold science, but can be strangely warm and affectionate about vehicles at the unfashionable and disfunctional end of the scale.

They smile cheerfully when they tell you how many times they broke down in their Lada, how many electrical glitches they found in their Jaguar and how close they felt to death every time they approached a corner in their Cortina Six.

Of course, such misty-eyed reminiscences come about only once a lemon has been despatched to the next owner or scrap merchant. Not when it is pouring with rain, the windows that aren't leaking are fogging up, you are already late because the alleged conveyance failed to respond to the turning of the key and the whole world is laughing anyway – even above the sound of the driving rain – because you were the sap who believed that paying an extortionate amount for a Holden Brougham really would make you look distinguished and irresistible to members of the opposite sex.

And there lies a delight of a book like this. It presents 65 more motoring millstones and allows you to run your eye over their curves (or in the case of the Quasar, complete lack of curves), share some of the excruciating experiences, snigger at the list of glitches, hiccups and oversights – and never have to own a single one of them.

INTRODUCTION • xi

Before getting into the cars themselves, it is worth quickly reflecting on exactly what type of motoring misery is covered in this book. As defined in its predecessor, *Lemon! 60 heroic failures of motoring*, the marks of outstanding failure include, but are not limited to:

- Catastrophic sales (illustrated in this volume by the Austin Freeway)
- Dastardly reliability (Chrysler Centura)
- Stupid names (Nissan Cedric)
- Bombastic styling (Daimler SP250)
- Terrifying flimsiness (Subaru 360)
- Uncalled-for longevity (Bristol Blenheim)
- Dicky science (Moller Skycar)
- Unrealised promise (Tucker 48)
- Deathly dullness (Toyota Corona)
- Corporate dodginess (Davis three-wheeler)
- Starting a trend that doesn't become one (Nash Metropolitan)
- The 'build it and they shall come' mindset (Panther Rio)
- The 'build it and they shall be injured' mindset (Ford Pinto)
- And all of the above (Trabant).

And the strangest thing of all? If asked if they would do it all again, many of these car-makers would say 'we wouldn't change a thing.'

Enjoy the ride. Turbulence is expected.

Tony Davis
July 2005

Jaguar XJ220

The fattest cat

In the late 1980s a vast number of people seemed to be in possession of a vast quantity of money. And by a quirk of financial history, this new wealth – apparently created out of nothing – had been distributed in perfectly inverse proportion to taste and restraint.

What better opportunity to launch the widest, ugliest, most ostentatious, altogether stupid Jaguar of all time?

From the moment this car – known as the XJ220 – was first shown in 1988, potential buyers were hammering on the door. Never mind that it was going to cost £415,554 ex-factory, was so wide it wouldn't fit down many roads, so powerful it was totally impractical in traffic and so highly strung it would need to be shipped back to headquarters regularly for obscenely expensive, racing car-style servicing. Within 48 hours of the announcement of 'limited edition' production, 1500 people had put up their hands for the 350 cars scheduled to be built.

These people either believed they needed one (they didn't) or that it would go up in value (it wouldn't). Those who got in first paid a 10 per cent deposit (roughly AU$100,000), while others forked out even more to buy a place from someone already in the queue. Behind this daft scenario, which was all to end in tears, there was a fair bit of cutting, chopping and changing within the Coventry cathouse.

The original show-car had featured a 6.2 L V12 and all-wheel drive. By the time specifications of the production version had been fixed, the XJ220 had a 3.5 L V6 (a development of the one fitted to the Metro 6R4 Rally car years before), and this powered only the rear wheels. Nonetheless, the production version boasted 404 kW and 642 Nm, plus the ability to rocket from rest to 100 km/h in under 4 seconds, and to 160 km/h in under 8 seconds.

The XJ name was designed to bring to mind the XK120 model and the stillborn XJ13 racer. The '220' was the projected top speed in miles per hour (equating to 354 km/h), making the XJ220 the world's fastest production car. Except the real top speed proved at least 7 mph short and the later, greater (but equally unsuccessful) McLaren F1 was soon to blow the Jaguar and other 'world's fastest car' aspirants into the weeds.

The XJ220 was 2.22 metres wide, a fraction under 5 metres long and weighed 1470 kg. Each of the four tyres was unique (so there was no spare), and each tyre cost about the same as a

second-hand car. At the press launch a journalist from *The Guardian* grabbed the wrong gear at high speed and, depending on whose report you believe, did damage worth thousands or tens of thousands of pounds. He wasn't the only one who had difficulty controlling this fearsomely quick, cumbersome and harsh machine.

Autocar magazine said the engine sounded like 'a pail of nuts and bolts being poured through a Magimix'. In short, the XJ220 was not the sort of thing that the fashion designers and rock stars who had ordered it were even slightly likely to enjoy driving.

Worse still, the production run didn't begin until July 1992, by which stage the economy had turned, the McLaren F1 had been unveiled, and so many buyers were so keen not to proceed they were willing to walk away from their substantial deposits. That wasn't good enough for Jaguar, which called in the lawyers to force completion. Many prospective buyers had already gone broke in the downturn, or simply refused to supply the balance, citing such things as the changed mechanical specifications. Settlements were reached, but it was a miserable business all around.

And how collectable was this so-called instant classic? A dozen or so years after the launch, a pristine example with low kilometres would struggle to fetch a quarter the original price. And did anyone feel sorry for the clots who had bought them new? Not bloody likely.

Prenvic

We know this car was built in Belgrade in 1959, we're just not entirely sure why. The best guess is that the Prenvic's curious diamond-pattern wheel arrangement was executed to win a bet. That, or to harness the advantages that have been claimed for the layout on the two or three other times people have been silly enough to adopt it. These include: a smaller turning circle (feasible), better aerodynamics (vaguely possible), more useable space (doubtful) and greater stability (you've got to be joking).

The styling was curious: a bit of Chrysler Airflow at the front, a tiny hint of filed-down Cadillac at the rear and a Sunbeam toaster in between. Sketchy mechanical details suggest the Prenvic's single front wheel turned in unison with its single rear wheel. Meanwhile, the other two wheels were cleverly positioned to be completely in the way of the doors.

Nissan Cedric

Of all the daft car names, and there have been plenty, none has been as widely discussed and popularly lampooned by Australians as the Cedric.

When the Cedric was first sold in Australia in 1963, it sported dog-leg windscreen pillars, fins and a few other hangovers of 1950s America that had only recently been erased from the best-selling Holden sedan. But far more important than any of that is the question of how the Japanese came up with such a silly moniker.

It was because Katsuji Kawamata, the Nissan supremo of the day, possessed a strange streak of Anglophilia. He believed 'Cedric' would bring to mind the image of a worldly, well-educated, upper-class English gentleman. Rather than, say, a lisping fop in a cravat with a slightly disturbing fondness for his mother.

Kawamata was also responsible for the Bluebird badge, perhaps inspired by the record-breaking antics of Sir Malcolm Campbell. And when he saw the Lerner-Loewe musical *My Fair Lady*, Kawamata-san decided the Pygmalion transformation of a dirty flower girl into a beautiful princess was exactly what his engineers had achieved when they put a roadster body on the chassis of a frumpy little Datsun truck. The Fairlady badge was born.

The origins of other Datsun/Nissan nomenclatural atrocities, such as Auster, Sunny, Violet, Gazelle, Stanza, Gloria, Sylvia, Cherry and Homy are less clear.

Cedric sales stopped in Australia around 1966, though the model line survives on the Japanese market as a boringly conventional car.

Chevrolet Corvair

The roll model

In the 1965 book *Unsafe at Any Speed*, Harvard Law School graduate Ralph Nader set out to paint General Motors as a corporation with a greater interest in profits than in the safety of its customers.

There was no better illustration, Nader proffered, than the rear-engined Chevrolet Corvair, which, he said, had a flawed, penny-pinching suspension system that caused drivers to lose control during turns and flip the car over.

GM responded in what it considered a sensible, practical and reasonable way. It hired private detectives to follow Nader in the hope of proving he was homosexual.

But why did GM produce such an unlikely 'compact' model in the first place? In a strange sort of way, its beginnings lay in

Germany before the war, because the unanticipated success of the VW Beetle in the USA during the 1950s convinced Chevrolet it needed a lighter car in its armoury. And if an air-cooled, horizontally opposed engine in the tail could work for the Germans, why not for the Americans?

Being Chevrolet, it decided that bigger was better, even if the Corvair was originally envisaged as a light car. So it ended up with a six-cylinder engine in the tail, albeit with a comparatively modest capacity (for the US) of 140 ci or 2.3 L. As well as being larger than the Beetle, the Corvair was a great deal more modern, with a monocoque body and aluminium engine. From a company better known for tarting up old designs with new bodywork than reengineering from the ground up, this was extraordinary stuff.

The first Corvair – released in late 1959 – broke other Detroit trends, with an austere interior and bodywork unadorned with fins or fields of chrome. It was offered as a two- or four-door. A van, station wagon and curious 'Rampside pickup' soon followed, then a convertible and a pioneering turbocharged engine option.

Nader's allegations concentrated on these early examples (1960-63 model year Corvairs), which he described as 'the one-car accident'. The Corvair certainly had a tendency to oversteer, or hang its tail out. Enthusiasts loved this, but it was not ideal for those who didn't adjust their driving style (most American cars tended to plough forward into a corner with huge understeer), or were lax about maintaining correct tyre pressures.

By the time Nader attacked, there were 103 Corvair lawsuits against GM, and Chevrolet had modified the suspension to control the rear 'tuck in' that *Unsafe at Any Speed* blamed for unpredictable handling. But the Ford Mustang was released in 1964 and did more to kill the Corvair than Nader ever could. It offered a powerful V8 and with fuel being so cheap who cared about the Corvair's greater fuel economy or mechanical sophistication?

A svelte new Corvair body for 1965 (pictured on previous page) was not enough to tackle Mustang, while the notorious (and bungled) Nader surveillance operation failed to rid GM of its 'consumer advocate' problem. GM President James Roche was forced to apologise to Nader before a Senate subcommittee, and the company eventually handed over US$425,000 for invasion of privacy. (It wasn't only homosexuality GM was looking for;

evidence tendered showed it would have been equally happy to prove Nader was a Communist or secret beneficiary of Corvair lawsuits.)

Like any good zealot, Nader used his newfound wealth to dig even deeper into the automotive industry – and the meat industry and almost every other potential infringer of consumer rights. In 1966, as a direct result of the Corvair affair, the US Federal Government announced its first National Traffic and Motor Vehicle Safety Act.

It is widely believed Chevrolet would have dropped the Corvair in 1967 for commercial reasons, but didn't want to be seen to be running. So the Corvair stumbled on until 1969, recording just 6000 sales in its final year, compared with nearly 330,000 in 1961. Buyers of the last examples needed to be coaxed with a credit towards the purchase of a future Chevrolet.

Meanwhile, none of the eight Corvair cases that went to trial were successful and the final twist came in 1972 when the National Highway and Traffic Safety Administration finally released its report into Nader's allegations. It concluded: 'The handling and stability performance of the 1960-63 Corvair does not result in an abnormal potential for loss of control or rollover, and it is at least as good as the performance of some contemporary vehicles, both foreign and domestic.'

Nader considered the report a whitewash. Corvair supporters had the bittersweet comfort of knowing the car had been pardoned after its execution.

Lightburn Zeta Sports

Extra light

Stylish, innovative, clever . . . there are many things the 1963 Lightburn Zeta Sedan wasn't, and these are but three. The thing it most wasn't, however, was practical.

Indeed, in this department the Zeta Sedan (we'll come to the Sports shortly) was the veritable *merde de la merde* of Australian cars, with a crude fibreglass body ugly enough to scare a gargoyle and a layout so daftly conceived that to access the rear load area the unlucky user had to open the front doors and remove the seats.

Would you buy a sports car from a company with such an automotive pedigree? That was the question asked of the Australian public in 1964 when the Lightburn Automotive Division announced its 'Sports' model.

The Zeta Sports came five years after the home-grown Goggomobil Dart and was remarkably similar in concept, right down to the tiny exterior dimensions, door-less body and rear-mounted two-stroke engine. That the moment for such a vehicle had passed might have been hinted at by the disappearance of the Dart from radar screens. But South Australian cement mixer manufacturer/would-be car magnate Harold Lightburn would not be deterred.

The Zeta's styling came from Michelotti of Italy via an English company that had built a similar vehicle (called the Frisky Sprint) in the late 1950s. And had deservedly gone belly-up.

At least the brochure for the Zeta Sports was exciting. If the Sedan was for the family man, the Sports was clearly created for the individual standing in the place where wild adventure and the swinging sixties met. Terms such as 'train-like cornering' and 'back-thumping acceleration' were liberally and ludicrously used. Yet – surprise, surprise – the new Zeta was no supercar. The only thing it could leap in a single bound was out of gear.

Which brings us to the mechanical aspects. Power was delivered by a '500 cc Continental two-stroke engine'. The term Continental was not a brand name but a generic term for something European that couldn't be described by the then-favourable term 'British'. The donk was a two-cylinder Sachs FMR powerplant from Germany, equipped with an integral four-speed gearbox. Although output was a modest 15.5 kW, the Sports weighed just 400 kg. Top speed was claimed as 75 mph (around 120 km/h) with the standing quarter mile coming up in 20.2 seconds.

The Sports sat on Mini-Minor-sized 10-inch wheels, had drum brakes, worm and peg steering and used a tubular chassis below the fibreglass shell. The single windscreen wiper on the driver's side was a good indication to stay at home when the weather was iffy.

Perhaps stung by reporting on the Zeta Sedan, Lightburn made no examples of the Sports available to the press. It's hard to gain any contemporary impressions as a result, but if the Sedan is anything to go by, assume the worst. The brochure term 'fully independent suspension', for example, probably indicated suspension that was fully independent of any attempt to control it.

The Zeta Sports body was bumper-less, with protruding headlights ready to take the brunt of any impact. These headlights presented other problems too, being too low to comply with New South Wales state legislation. The first solution

LIGHTBURN ZETA SPORTS • 13

attempted was to raise the suspension, but the ground-hugging Zeta couldn't be raised far enough, and so cars were delivered with an extra set of 'sports lights' bolted onto the guards above the normal ones. Sporty suddenly looked a great deal less sporty. Or to put it more frankly, ugly and silly became uglier and sillier.

If the Zeta Sports was an improvement over the Sedan, it was in the same way Ivan the Terrible was bettered by his little known successor, Ivan the Tolerable. That as many as 50 Zeta Sports models were produced is surprising. That Lightburn Automotive Division built its last Zeta of any description in 1965 is not.

Fiat Croma

Fix it again, Tony

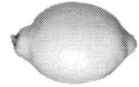

When announced in Australia in late 1987, the Croma was heralded as the first new Fiat in three years and the forerunner to a broad range of exciting new models.

History records that these exciting new models never arrived. Indeed, the unloved, unexciting and un-most-other-things-too Croma became the death of Fiat cars on the Australian market for the rest of the 20th century.

Problem one was that the Croma, armed with just four cylinders and 84 kW, cost $45,000. That was twice as much as it should have cost in an era when you could buy a superior Mazda 626 for $25,000 or, if you wanted to go Italian, an Alfa 75 for $35,000.

The good people of Fiat Australia, no strangers to loopy logic, said that such comparisons were unfair. The real competitors wore Mercedes-Benz and BMW badges. Why Fiat believed it had suddenly climbed 14 notches in the public perception is unclear, but Australians weren't buying the comparison. And they weren't buying the Croma.

The 2.0 L, front-drive Croma was Fiat's largest luxury model of the time and was described as a 'five-door prestige saloon'. The body was the handiwork of Giorgio Giugiaro and was a cross between a sedan and a hatchback. It looked clean and modern and was relatively roomy. The handling was quite good too, and ride comfort commendable. But a paltry 84 kW and 165 Nm propelling more than 1200 kg through a three-speed automatic gearbox was not going to get the heart racing. It was the build quality that did that.

At the media launch one car had a headlight assembly fall out under hard cornering. The engine of this writer's car stopped dead in the right lane in the middle of an overtaking manoeuvre. This was nearly as big a surprise as having found something the car was capable of overtaking.

In the Croma press kit, Fiat marketers predicted initial Australian sales of 200 Cromas a year, with the subsequent launch of a turbo version and the Tipo hatchback combining to give the company a 'significant share of the luxury market'.

The kit also contained pages and pages about the anti-corrosion measures (25 treatments using nine different processes, it said), adding that 43 per cent of the body was made of galvanised steel. That last statistic only served to make anyone who knew anything about Italian cars worry about the other 57 per cent.

Having decided to charge a moonshot premium for the Croma, Fiat promoted it with the slogan 'the affordable European alternative'. As time passed, the Croma became a more and more affordable European alternative. When press reports hit home, Fiat undertook a 'price action' and 'realigned the Croma's position within the market'. Which is to say, it cut the guts out of the asking price. The Croma became $35,000, then $25,000. People still weren't interested. Imports of all Fiats stopped soon afterwards.

Quasar

When the science of aerodynamics swept the world, it somehow missed Middlesex, England, where the Quasar was built in 1968.

This cubular hell was the work of a British automotive parts supplier, Universal Power Drives Ltd, and was based on a design by Quasar Khann, a North Vietnamese engineer living in Paris.

Six was the magic number, the Quasar being 6 feet wide, 6 feet long and 6 feet tall. It could also seat exactly that same number of adults. The Quasar made use of sliding doors, apparently so the occupants – if not already deep-fried by the sun or permanently stuck to the transparent PVC inflatable plastic seats – could park the vehicle in tight spaces and then exit easily. There was one sliding door on each side and one at the front, so presumably the Quasar could also double as a patio/entertaining area.

Universal Power Drives boasted its 'exciting new creation' would become a popular city vehicle as it could turn in half the space of a family sedan. Looking at the shape and high centre of gravity, one suspects it could roll in half the time, too.

The 'body-work' was manufactured from Triplex safety glass, and that single windscreen wiper looks capable of sweeping at least 3 per cent of it.

Power came from a British Motor Company 1100 engine, placed in the rear. Universal Power Drives described the top speed as 'restricted to 50 mph'. In a car that isn't much, but in a glorified shower recess it sounds positively frightening. Production was limited. Very.

Austin X6

The Pre-76

Forget 'The Big Three'. It's now 'The Big Four'. From the makers of Rover, Daimler and Jaguar, here's the most advanced family car ever built in Australia: a sophisticated six-cylinder model that will have Holden, Ford and Chrysler shaking in their boots.

That was the rallying cry for Leyland Australia's locally developed Austin X6 sedan, which replaced the four-cylinder Austin 1800 in 1970.

Available in Tasman form or as the more upmarket – or less downmarket – Kimberley model, the X6 was front-wheel drive. Its 2.2 L OHC engine was placed east–west, perhaps the first time an inline six had been shoehorned in that direction. This arrangement required a separate electric fan, another rarity for the era. There was also full-flow ventilation, newfangled hazard

lights (later to be popularly known as 'park-anywhere lights') and a variety of other fancy features. The enigmatic styling was local too. Crisp and clean from some angles, it had an almost rear-engined Eastern European look about it from others.

Output was 76 kW in the one-carb Tasman and 86 kW in the twin-carb Kimberley. Either could be had with a four-speed manual or three-speed automatic transmission. Handling was fairly impressive, so was the ride.

Liking it so far? Well, now the bad news. Like many Leyland products, this was a concept with a lot to commend it. The failure was in the execution. The X6 was short on the lowdown torque that made the Aussie big sixes so effortless to drive. And on a marketing level, British-oriented family car-buyers still considered there to be something a bit weird and Continental about front-wheel drive.

Smaller than its 'big six' competitors (shoulder room was especially tight), the X6 was no cheaper to run. It was particularly heavy on fuel. The seats were poor (seat comfort had been a strong point of its 1800 predecessor), and the X6 had a duff cable-operated gearchange, controls and switches that worked slowly or refused altogether, and wipers that didn't sweep the whole screen. Oh, and hard-to-reach switches, poorly positioned pedals, steering that was heavy and kicked back savagely and suspension that went thump in the night and day.

To add to all this, there was grim build quality and miserable reliability. The X6 tended to stall at idle, overheat or just refuse to work. Leyland had made bold predictions about market penetration. But sales never even reached 'modest' and, far from shaking in their boots, the executives of Holden, Ford and Valiant registered not even a minor tremor in their collective footwear.

The X6 boasted 85 per cent local content. Thanks to the use of existing Austin 1800 body structures and suspension, Leyland engineers developed the entire car for just $4.5 million. Today it could cost that much to develop a new set of bumper bars. Mind you, a good set of bumper bars might bring more pleasure than anything with Tasman or Kimberley badges.

In June 1972, Mark II versions of the X6 twins brought many much-needed minor improvements. Unfortunately though, the new versions failed to bring any of the much-needed major improvements.

In the meantime, the rear-wheel drive Marina had been launched in an ill-fated attempt to satisfy those suspicious of front-drive complexity. But bigger and better things were in the wings. Yes, the company was readying for market an entirely new family sedan which would totally transform the company's fortunes: the Leyland P76.

Bond Bug

Perhaps the oddest car of 1970 came out of England and was known as the Bond Bug. Designed by Czech-born Tom Karen, it was an attempt to adapt the cheap but dowdy English three-wheeler – mostly used by invalids – into a vehicle for the hip and happening.

However, the hip and happening knew a dog when they saw it, and production lasted just four years.

All examples of the Bug (the name was at least as clever as AMC's Gremlin and just as prescient) were painted in a garish shade of orange known as Tangerine, with the black writing on the tail supposedly giving the aura of a sponsored racing car.

Ford Cortina Six

On the nose

It was in September 1972 that Ford Australia added a six-cylinder engine to its Cortina model, completely transforming a nimble medium-sized sedan.

What it was transformed into was a nose-heavy, fuel gulping horror with hideously heavy steering and handling that occupied that slender niche between bad and bloody awful.

OK, it was quick in a straight line, but so is a brick dropped from a window. And the dismal build quality that had been a hallmark of Cortinas received no real attention during the makeover. It just became a faster pig.

Why was it so? The story went something like this: in the early 1970s Ford Australia was leading the medium car segment with its locally made (but English-sourced) four-cylinder Cortina. It was nice work while Ford could get it, but it wasn't hard to see the situation was temporary. The Japanese had adopted the devious policy of building cars that didn't constantly break down or have things fall off them, and it was only a matter of time before such skulduggery hurt the, um, more traditionally crafted Cortina.

Ford's solution was to take itself out of the race. By adding a six-cylinder engine to the options list for the TC series it moved its car into a different segment. The extra cylinders would differentiate Cortina from the primarily four-cylinder Japanese competition (and hopefully inject some excitement into the range). It would also enable Ford to directly take on Holden's Torana six, a local model that had pioneered the concept of

combining the interior room of a small four-cylinder car with the thirst and expense of a family-sized model.

There was an aspect to the Cortina Six the bean counters particularly liked: the re-used Falcon mechanical components were mostly cheaper than the imported ones used in the four-cylinder Cortina. Yet a six could always command a higher retail price than a four. After all, it's two more.

Cortina Six buyers had a choice between the 200 and 250 Falcon engines, with 3.3 L and 4.1 L respectively. To help justify the extra price, they received a 'power bulge' in the bonnet (it wasn't entirely for show – the Falcon engine was taller as well as longer) plus that very 1970s symbol of prestige motoring, quad headlights. And if Cortina buyers really, really wanted to impress the neighbours, they could order a white vinyl roof.

Putting the six in the Cortina required a lot of re-engineering. The same amount of effort might have been better spent improving the woeful build quality of the original version. An updated TD six-cylinder Cortina was produced from October 1974, then from July 1977 the completely new-look Cortina TE was available. Both series had the six-cylinder engine available alongside the four.

By 1981 high costs had ensured that the English experiment was all but over. Australian Cortina production was discontinued and Ford played the if-you-can't-beat-them-join-them game and switched to Japan for its medium car. With the Mazda-based but Australian-assembled Telstar, Ford once again enjoyed the rarefied air at the top of the medium car segment. In the process it proved it hadn't needed a six, just a well-built four.

Fiat ESV 1500

ESV was a buzz word of 1970. Not that it was a word, as such. It was an acronym for Experimental Safety Vehicle, and came about because in that year the USA's Department of Transportation responded to the new safety lobby by coining the term, publishing a series of ESV guidelines and recommending that car-makers set to work on them if they wanted to sell cars in the USA in the future.

The general rules seemed to be these: get an undistinguished car, restyle it to make it even uglier, cover all the sharp bits inside and out with thick padding, then devise a system of interior safety webs, belts, buckles and harnesses more convoluted than the wiring diagram of the London Underground.

Most ESVs made you grateful that looks can't kill. This Fiat effort was at least as silly as most, being unsightly enough to be unsaleable, impossibly heavy and too expensive to mass-produce. Mind you, being a Fiat of the 1970s, its main safety feature would have been that it spent most of its time off the road being repaired.

Subaru 360

The sub-VeeDub

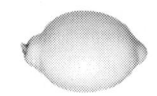

The late 1950s and early 1960s brought a flood of Japanese micro-cars. These included the Mazda 360, Suzulight 360 and Mitsubishi 500, each providing a reminder that before Japan made cars that were reliable, well-built and stylish, they made cars that were un-, badly and less than.

The forerunner of the Japanese minis, though, was the Subaru 360, created when someone at Fuji Heavy Industries (FHI) discovered Japan's 'micro vehicle' legislation – created to make motorcycles and three-wheeled delivery vans affordable – could be adapted for cars.

The Subaru 360 appeared in March 1958. It was a radical four-wheeler that sneakily complied with all the micro laws by having an overall length less than 3 metres (shorter than the original Mini Minor), a weight below 350 kg and a sub-360 cc engine. Buyers could use a cheaper restricted driving licence and would pay about one-tenth the road tax of those buying a full-size vehicle.

The Subaru 360 was designed to be just big enough to carry a family of four, while offering all-weather protection. The instrumentation consisted solely of a speedometer, the turn-signals were manual blinkers and the four-speed gearbox lacked a proper synchromesh. The doors were of the forward-opening 'suicide' type, the body a mishmash of poorly fitting panels, while the bottom of the rear wheels tucked in under the tail to make sure the finished product never looked quite secure in the upright position. But the 360 was cheap.

Many considered the Subaru, with its rack-and-pinion steering, torsion bar suspension and air-cooled, rear-mounted donk, to be a shrunken VW Beetle. However, the Subaru had only two cylinders and its microscopic engine – a two-stroke with a built-in propensity for overheating and seizing – screamed its head off to produce just 16 bhp (11.5 kW).

The Subaru beat the Mini Minor with the least commendable thing about the Mini Minor: 10-inch wheels. These could disappear into things larger vehicles didn't even consider to be potholes.

FHI used the name Subaru (rather than Rabbit, the name of its scooters), taking it from the Japanese term for the cluster of six stars known to Australians as the constellation Taurus. It managed to build just 604 examples in the first year, but convertible and light commercial derivatives joined the line-up as production improved. Subaru also offered a 423 cc engine in export markets, including Australia, where 72 were sold.

In the USA the paths of Subaru and an entrepreneur named Malcolm Bricklin crossed in a fashion as colourful and ill-fated as one would expect from the man who would later give his name to one of the world's truly incompetent sports cars. Bricklin first imported Rabbit scooters, then marketed the 360 sedan under the unlikely slogan of 'Cheap and Ugly Does It'. By US standards, the Subaru 360 was so small it should have been labelled 'Not for Individual Sale'. Yet Bricklin discovered that same tininess exempted it from US emission and safety regulations. It was a much-needed exemption.

The timing was interesting, for if you were to create a list of everything that the Americans looked for in a car in 1968, the Subaru would have lined up perfectly with the 'not required' column. Americans thought the VW was minuscule – a smaller-scale replica made no sense at all. America's *Road & Track* magazine stated the Subaru was 'of uncommon ugliness' before recording a dismally slow 0-to-50 mph acceleration time of 36 seconds (the car wouldn't make 60 mph).

Bricklin made a song and dance of the frugal fuel use, but that was an advantage almost anywhere but the US, where fuel was so cheap that Oldsmobile and others happily marketed cars with engines 20 times as large as the Subaru's. The American lack of interest in the 360 became even more pronounced when *Consumer Reports* magazine labelled it 'the most unsafe car in America'.

With Subaru's six stars in freefall and 1000 unsold cars in stock, Bricklin started FasTrack International, with the aim of franchising a $1-per-lap motor racing theme park. Each franchise came with 10 Subaru 360s, presumably to remind budding racing drivers that motor sport is dangerous. When FasTrack achieved all the success it deserved, Bricklin slid out of the whole operation and embarked on the path to losing millions of other people's dollars building a 'gullwing' sports car bearing his own name.

Meanwhile, for all its faults, the little Subaru stayed in production until 1970. By then, one million had been sold, mostly in Japan.

Datsun 280ZX

The Z-Z-Z car

Once upon a time there was a long, low and exciting coupe badged as the Datsun 240Z. America's *Road & Track* magazine called it 'the most significant sports car of the '70s'. But in just a few years, Datsun's best and brightest had turned this 'Zed One' into the 280ZX.

Hundreds of millions of yen and thousands of hours of intense development had turned a light, stylish, agile, quick and affordable coupe into one that was heavy, unattractive, lumbering, slow and expensive.

The 240Z was styled by ex-Studebaker designer Albrecht Graf Goertz and released in 1970. It was half the price of the aging E-Type Jaguar, but considerably more than half the car. The Zed's top speed of around 200 km/h and standing quarter time of

16.7 seconds left competitors such as the MGB in the shade. Likewise its handling.

The revamped 260Z, released in 1974, provided a signal of what was to come. Every major statistic had increased – including capacity, power and weight – while an additional two-plus-two variant (which is to say a semi-four-seater) saw the overall length blow out even further. But it was the 280ZX of March 1979 that totally lost the plot. Those early Zed cars had shown admirable restraint with their interior and exterior decoration, but this one gave way to chrome galore, chintzy body decorations and seats covered in the sort of velour you'd find in a really crook nightclub.

The Zed was now two-plus-two only and Datsun was using the term 'personal coupe', as if no longer game to say 'sports car'. With an Australian launch price of $17,500, the 280ZX was the most expensive Japanese car of its day.

The bonnet seemed to go on forever. It's hard to say why, since it hid an inline six-cylinder engine which produced just 98 kW and was expected to propel nearly 1300 kg, usually via a three-speed automatic. The dramatic acceptance of the slushbox option (the majority of Zeds were now thus equipped), along with the presence of power windows, power mirrors and featherweight power-assisted steering, showed that the Zed car was pitched at a very different buyer. The main reason for the switch from lean-and-mean to obese-and-serene was that, with 80 per cent of Zeds going to the USA, the car had been increasingly tailored to the, er, unique tastes of that market.

In 1980 a T-bar roof was added, making the 280ZX a sort of semi-demi-convertible. And even heavier. A brochure photo was captioned: 'T-Bar roof stores easily'. It showed two vinyl wrapped panels occupying the entire width and length of the boot.

By 1982 the 280ZX was now officially a 'Nissan' and was

marketed as 'the only luxury hatchback coupe available with a targa roof'. Sports car – what's that? Launched in 1984, the 300ZX V6 was a bit more agile than the 280ZX but was still a car more for a mid-life crisis than a lap dash. A remake of the 300ZX for the 1990s captured just a little of the former glory but by then the price was stratospheric. The Zed car then disappeared completely until Renault took management control of the bankrupt Nissan company and revived the badge.

Lada 110

After punishing the Russian people and a few foreigners for more than a decade with the dire and distressing Lada Samara (also known as 'the 1300', 'the Volonte' and 'the cause of the blockage'), the pioneers of Total Quality Mismanagement and Not-Quite-in-Time production supplemented it with an all-new model.

It was the Lada 110, launched in 1995. Lada claimed the 110 incorporated design suggestions from Porsche. If so, they must have been suggestions along the lines of 'Ve vould not do it like zat, if ve vere you.'

To many car-buyers, the sign of quality is a car with doors that shut with a resounding clunk. In keeping with the quality Lada buyers expected, the 110 had doors that opened with resounding clunk. And a photo is one thing, but a Lada dashboard in the plastic is worth more than a thousand words.

Hillman Imp

Frailty, thy name is Hillman

The car was called Imp and every second advertisement and newspaper article used words such as IMPressive and IMPortant. Closer to the mark, however, was IMPrudent. Because although the Imp was British small car innovation at its most venturesome, it was also financial suicide.

The whole sorry saga started in the mid-1950s, when The Rootes Group (known for its solid Hillman and Humber models) commenced a 'what if?' small-car design exercise. Its directors had earlier made it clear they had little interest in economy models, and were among those who had so famously turned down the Volkswagen company after the war. It was little surprise, therefore, that this new exercise produced more talk and paperwork than firm proposals.

HILLMAN IMP • 35

Everything changed with the success of the Mini Minor. Rootes' directors did an about-face and a small car became a big priority. In a breathless three-year period, the design of a radical Hillman small car was finalised and an all-new plant was built in Scotland to manufacture it. In May 1963 the car hit the market amid enormous excitement. The Imp seemed as radical as the Mini and was equally sporting. And while the Mini was front-engined, front-drive, the Imp was the complete opposite. Furthermore, it featured such things as a motor sport-derived all-aluminium engine and a hatchback-style lift-up rear window.

In the UK, 20,000 orders were taken in the first two days. And when the car was launched in Australia in early 1964, buyers seemed equally taken with the newest Hillman.

However, the exciting promise of those early days quickly faded. As the Imp demonstrated more than its share of teething problems and design limitations, the Mini's success seemed to grow and grow, casting a huge shadow which all but obscured the littlest Hillman.

The dictionary defines an imp as a little devil or demon, or a mischievous child. Hillman's version lived up to its name, ungratefully helping to bankrupt its creators. (In 1964 the haemorrhaging Rootes Group was snapped up by Chrysler Corporation.)

Technically, the Imp was nothing if not interesting. The body was a fraction bigger than the Mini's, while its 875 cc engine was produced in collaboration with Coventry Climax (the company that had produced world-beating Cooper and Lotus racing engines) and laid over at a 45-degree angle, lowering the centre of gravity and making room for a modest luggage compartment above.

The Imp had sharp handling (though with an inelegant tendency to cock its front wheels in the air at speed), a nice gear-shift and effective brakes. However, the recommended tyre pressures (15 psi in the front, 30 in the rear) gave some idea that it wasn't a car with perfect, 50-50 weight distribution. There were other gripes. The Imp was available only in drab colours, it lacked front flipper windows (then considered a necessity), and was noisy and unduly susceptible to side winds. Quality was a lucky dip. The Scots building it were mainly new to the car industry and the design was undercooked anyway. Many Imps demonstrated a voracious hunger for throttle cables, water pumps and other things not generally regarded as 'consumables'. The engine's tendency to overheat and warp became legendary.

The quality story became even worse as the 1960s progressed. Sales continued to fall and the bean counters battled the situation by cutting costs rather than improving the vehicle. Nonetheless, the Imp stumbled on for the rest of the decade, finally being put out to pasture in Australia in 1970. Amazingly, it continued in the UK until 1976.

In 1978, Hillman – a brand dating to before World War I – joined the enormously long list of famous British car marques to fall from the sky. Once again, pilot error seemed solely responsible.

Toyota Corona 'Starfire'

Wake-up call

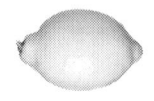

The Corona formula was always simple: mediocre performance and reasonable equipment levels wrapped in bodywork so bland it defied non-description.

Although its main appeal was to people who didn't like cars, and the age of the average buyer was almost into three figures, the Corona was reliability personified. Or autofied. Since appearing on the Australian market in 1964, it had shown a remarkable ability to keep keeping on with almost no TLC.

The 1979 model was billed as the first all-Australian Corona. That was something most people had never thought they needed. Toyota executives, however, had to meet strict local content requirements and needed to build an Australian Corona badly. They built one very badly indeed.

The main problem was that Toyota Manufacturing Australia (TMC) decided to whack in a Holden-built Starfire engine, despite severe reservations about the content of its character. Holden had done the hard sell on Toyota because it needed more volume for an engine then fitted only to its Sunbird, an unwanted variant of the moribund Holden Torana. The 1.9 L Starfire engine – soon popularly known as the Misfire – was based on the Commodore six-cylinder donk, itself a relic of the 1960s, and by now well and truly outclassed. To create a four, two cylinders were lopped off and a cornucopia of new quirks and foibles added in.

Not that that there seemed anything much amiss with the 1979 Corona at first. The reviews were reasonable, sales were strong. The Starfire-engined Corona proved to be an acquired distaste.

TMC had clearly been nervous from the off, fitting several Japanese parts (such as a new camshaft) before launch-day to try to improve things. It wasn't enough: the Starfire tended to vibrate (a shock for Corona drivers, who were normally in a sound sleep), various parts failed and Toyota dealers became reacquainted with oil leaks. Those same dealers soon discovered that whereas boring dependability had always done well for them, it was much harder to sell boring undependability.

Back at TMC head office, engineers responded to Misfire mishaps by fitting their own gaskets, valves, valve springs and water pump. Soon there were 50 different Japanese components fitted to an engine that Toyota had outsourced in the belief it would save money. And if a lack of reliability wasn't enough, customers also received miserable fuel economy, thereby completely defeating the purpose of buying of what they perceived as a small and efficient Japanese car.

As sales slid, there was an energetic renegotiation of the five-year supply contract and the Corona had a Toyota-built engine back under its featureless nose by 1983.

Moller Skycar

Ever since man has been able to drive and fly, inventors have tried to produce a vehicle that will do both. It's been mostly the stuff of meat and pastry in the firmament, though in 1951 the Aerocar achieved limited success. Never mind that its wings had to be carried in a trailer about as long as a small bus, or that nobody bought it. It could fly, after a fashion, and drive, after another.

Canadian-raised Dr Paul Moller has spent more than 30 years and anything up to $150 million working on his George Jetson-like, eight-engined, vertical take-off Skycar. He even brought it to Australia in 2001 to talk about (rather than demonstrate) its cloud-hopping, kilometre-eating capabilities, which he claims include 600 km/h cruising with hatchback economy.

Despite decades of hype – the first order was taken in 1974 – the Skycar has never flown for more than a minute, and then only on the end of a rope. Still, Moller reckons he'll untether his creation and hit 600 km/h soon. At present only one Skycar exists but Moller says once production hits half a million units a year the price will come down to that of a mid-sized luxury car. The biggest risk at that point will be a herd of pigs pulling out from behind a cloud and overtaking you.

Honda Z

Scream de la scream

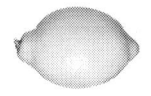

Anyone who took even a brief look at the minuscule Honda Z would be hard pressed to believe that the company that built it would one day be a dominant force in motor sport, and a respected maker of large luxury cars and Ferrari-like sports machines.

Indeed, the casual observer might very well have laughed out loud and taken a bet on how quickly the Honda car would join such other Japanese automotive failures as the Cony Guppy, Paddle PD33 and Flying Feather. There was, after all, something frankly ridiculous about the Honda's combination of zany curves, upswept waistline, television screen rear window, sports car interior and lawn-mower sized engine.

Launched in Australia in late 1971, the front-drive Z looked as outrageous as other sports machines on the road at the time, yet was under 3 metres long and only 1.3 metres wide. The Z was based on the mechanical components of the Honda Scamp, a sort of Japanese Mini Minor first seen down under in 1968.

The Scamp set new benchmarks for noisiness, yet had surprised people with the performance it produced from an engine less than half the size of the Mini unit (the Scamp had just 356 cc up its mechanical sleeve). As with the Scamp, the Z owed its existence to the Japanese tax regime, which allowed special concessions to sub-360 cc, sub-3-metre 'micro' cars.

With a healthy dose of 1970s prose, *Australian Motor Manual* called the Z the 'the most way-out micro yet'. *Modern Motor*

explained the Z was 'basically a Scamp with a groovy body', adding 'the cheeky little bomb takes the impudence stakes by a long nose'. Honda itself had yet to master hyperbole, a fact shown by a brochure which boasted a 'quite spacious interior' and 'quite enough power to assure adequate speeds'. There was also the cautious 'If you consider it carefully, you're quite likely to find this Honda can fill your motoring needs most adequately.'

Australians asked what the Z stood for. Local importers arbitrarily decided on 'Zot' and local advertisements urged people to 'Zot down the road to buy a Honda Z'.

The Z weighed only 525 kg. Its shrieking two-cylinder engine revved to nearly 10,000 rpm and cranked out 23 kW (not bad from a third of a litre, but not much with four aboard). If you could stand the noise and didn't overload it, the Z could zip comfortably along with the traffic, reaching a top speed of 105 km/h. But it took its time to get there. The standing quarter mile required around 25 seconds – and you still had to wait another 5 seconds or so to reach 100 km/h.

The early Zs had air-cooling but a water-cooled, twin-carb engine was later introduced. Equipment levels were high, though the quality and reliability that would eventually make Japanese cars legendary was still far from a standard inclusion. Many Honda Zs tended to rattle their panels loose and even unglued their back windows. And when mechanical wear reared its ugly head, the cost of fixing the relatively complex powerplant often outstripped the value of the car (the Lilliputian engine case also contained the gearbox and differential).

Despite this, at a bargain $1679 the Z quickly became the most successful Honda four-wheeler sold in Australia up to that time. This was a minor achievement if you look at its oddball forebears, but it was nonetheless the start of bigger and better things. In early 1973 Honda launched the Civic and intensified its drive to become more sophisticated and mainstream. The company suddenly seemed embarrassed by the cheerfully goofy image presented by the Z, which was still on sale. Australian Z sales stopped before the year was out.

Zil

No A-to-Z of bad cars can be complete without the fortuitously named Zil (although Yugoslavia's Zastava Yugo and the Ukraine's Zaz brand also do their best to fall off the back-end of the alphabet).

The Zil company commenced operation in Moscow in 1936 and for many years provided the cars of choice for Politburo members. The ludicrously large Zil 4104 and even more breathtakingly obese 41047 made it into the 21st century, each powered by a 7.7 L V8 and weighing 3.6 and 4.2 tonnes respectively. Although the bent-eight was ancient and fed by carburettor, the maker claimed the rather impressive power and torque figures of 232 kW and 608 Nm.

Pictured here is a 1970 model, which a Tass news agency caption called a 'light passenger car'. Although it looked like pure Americana of the 1950s, by the mid-1980s Zil models had been heavily updated – to look more Dallas motorcade, circa 1963.

It appears that Zil production finally spluttered to a halt around 2003.

Holden Piazza

Italian for dud

There was the usual bumpf: talk of 'bringing a new level of excitement and style to the sports car market', extensive use of words such as 'exclusive' and 'sophisticated', and detailed tables to show that the newcomer was not only superior to the competition but also better value for money.

But behind all the Piazza press launch pizzazz, Holden executives must have been very nervous about trying to charge a big premium in 1986 for a vehicle based on a show-car from 1979, and using mechanicals from the rear-drive Isuzu Gemini of the mid-1970s.

The Piazza had been first produced in Japan in 1981. Why Australians waited five years for it was a mystery. Why they eventually received it was another. It was the first turbocharged passenger car sold by Holden and, at $34,500, the dearest yet to wear lion-and-stone badges. Fittingly, it was launched on 1 April.

Built in Japan by Isuzu, the Piazza was styled in Italy by Giugiaro with a sharp-edged, clean-lined body that weathered the years a lot better than such contemporaries as the Nissan Gazelle and Mitsubishi Cordia. But the body was the high-point, and the price-tag reflected a delusion by bean counters that a Holden that looked exotic and European could command an exotic European price.

Supposedly justifying the high sticker price were a *Star Wars*-style digital instrument cluster and a single windscreen wiper that increased its speed as the car accelerated. The 2.0 L SOHC engine was turbocharged and intercooled. It developed 110 kW and 225 Nm, both figures considered impressive in 1986. And, although harsh at high revs, this engine was torquey down low and smooth in an age when most turbos were anything but.

That's it for the good news. A mid-1970s chassis (and not even a good one) combined with a lively turbo engine was a recipe for misery. Nervous wasn't the word. Keeping the front wheels sticking to the road at speed was hard work (and at speed in rain, near impossible), while the rear end was all over the shop at the slightest provocation.

'Mightily disappointed,' said *Wheels* magazine. 'Bump steer, roll oversteer, understeer and alarming nose dive under brakes – it's all there.' The Piazza also lacked the ability to cope with anything less than a perfectly smooth surface. The ride was pig-rough and the collection of binnacles and pods that made up Piazza's dated dashboard rattled, squeaked and shimmied.

When the car was universally panned, Holden slashed $5000 off the price and refunded those very few people who had put down $34,500. This cut was made at a time when other Japanese sporties were rising dramatically in price, but it didn't get things moving. Neither did a comprehensive suspension reworking that transformed the car's road manners from atrocious to merely very bad. When *Motor* magazine called Piazza 'the most frightening car we have tested in a long time', it was talking about the improved version.

Holden's head of marketing, John Loverage, had boasted that 'Piazza's sophisticated, hi-tech image will create a "halo effect" over the entire Holden range.' It didn't. The Piazza was the company's most dismal sales flop and the model was quickly, quietly and wisely phased out.

Scamp

The two-seater, fibreglass-bodied Scamp is described in some circles as 'the last car solely conceived, designed and built in Scotland'.

Don't be fooled by the Cyclops eye and trinket styling, these people were serious. They thought they could take on the Mini Minor and Hillman Minx with an electric vehicle possessing just two seats, a miserable range of 30 km between charges and a price that was dangerously close to that of a real car.

The Scamp was designed to keep Scottish Aviation engineers busy after production of the twin-engined Prestwick Pioneer aeroplane came to an end, circa 1964. Finance was provided by the Electricity Council, which intended to sell the Scamp next to washing machines and light fittings in its high-street showrooms.

Stirling Moss, who was no stranger to linking his name with British cars with plenty of room for improvement, loaned or rented some kind words, but it wasn't enough. The Scamp was absolutely flat biscuit at 60 km/h on the level, with one occupant. The old-fashioned lead-acid batteries – wired up to a salvaged aeroplane starter motor – were expensive to replace and needed recharging far too frequently.

Worse still, the Electricity Council insisted on independent safety evaluation by the Motor Industry Research Association. When the Scamp's suspension collapsed during the tests that followed, it made many people glad they weren't 5000 metres up in something else made by Scottish Aviation. The rather spectacular failure also led to the Electricity Commission unplugging itself from the project.

Scottish Aviation continued for a while, but only 11 or 12 Scamps were made.

Oldsmobile Toronado

Trailing from the front

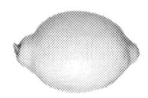

It was heralded in 1966 as 'America's car of the year' by no lesser authority than *Motor Trend*, which also raved about its handling. Others also gushed profusely, calling it the most desirable Oldsmobile of all time.

Maybe there was something in the air (it was the 1960s). Maybe aficionados of the brand were just over-excited about the first new mainstream front-drive US car since the Cord of the 1930s. But exactly what the cheer squad was thinking is hard to say, because to love the Toronado generally involved falling head over heels with the body – which many did, despite its wallowing tail and front guards designed to neatly slice pedestrians in two – and ignoring almost everything else.

The Toronado was claimed to be the largest front-wheel drive car ever, a very curious achievement. The main advantage of powering the front rather than the rear wheels is to improve packaging efficiency. Sure, the cabin floor of the Toronado was flat because there was no driveshaft running fore to aft, but considering the limousine-like 5.36 metre overall length, the interior should have been about the size of an Imperial ballroom.

Alas, much of the potential passenger room was lost in those huge overhangs, while a stunted two-door cabin with sloping roofline squandered most of what was left. The rear seat occupants put up with leg room crampingly similar to that of another front-wheel drive car, the Mini Minor, while the driver endured two massive blind spots due to those mighty rear pillars. As for harnessing front-drive's weight advantages, the Toronado tipped the scales at only a tiny shade less than 2 tonnes.

Like the Cord, the Toronado had its headlights secreted behind covers. There were strange 'power bulges' over the wheel arches. 'Toronado is all man – right down to that man sized trunk,' cried one ad. What it didn't mention is that even men who were all men objected to the ridiculous weight of the massive doors and within a year or so of the car's release the company had to introduce a 'built-in assist' mechanism to help open and close them.

After congratulating the buyer on choosing the Toronado, the owner's manual remarked 'never has there been a car with so many distinguishing characteristics.' One of these characteristics was high temperatures under that massive hood, which led to a spate of engine fires. Another was diabolical handling. If the Toronado had great road manners (as suggested by the US press), then it was only when compared with other Oldsmobiles.

With such bulk over the front wheels, the Toronado did more than chew up tyres at a fearsome rate. It lifted understeer – the tendency to plough forward in a corner – to a new art. And with such a vast engine and larduous kerb weight, what did engineers use to stop the Toronado? Yes, feeble drum brakes all round.

The bonnet that went on forever housed a gargantuan 7 L (425 ci) V8. This fed its power to the front wheels via a complex split transmission system with the three-speed auto box under the left cylinder bank and a torque converter mounted on the back of the engine. The two were connected by a chain and sprocket. The system was reputedly based on a patent purchased from Ford – which couldn't make it work. And because Oldsmobile buyers ultimately didn't care whether the front or rear wheels were being driven, and the Toronado took no other advantage of its chosen mechanical configuration, all the expense and complexity was for nothing.

Fuel consumption was everything you'd expect with a 7 L engine driving through a slushy three-speed auto. Despite this, more than 40,000 Toronados were sold in the first year, and a few came to Australia, where *Sports Car World* magazine described the wet-weather handling as lousy and the braking as diabolical.

When US sales dropped by about half in year two, Oldsmobile invoked the time honoured car-makers' solution: when in trouble, increase the engine size and add more chrome. For 1968, Toronados were fitted with 7.4 L engines.

And for the 1969 model year, front discs became standard, lifting the Toronado's braking performance so dramatically it now scraped the underside of 'barely adequate'. The 1970 model dispensed with the hidden headlights, opting instead for four round lights set within the grille. Words completely fail to explain the ugliness of this new styling treatment, which left the Toronado cross-eyed and permanently squinting.

The Toronado nameplate was phased out in the early 1990s. In 2004 the entire Oldsmobile brand, which dated back to 1897 and had been part of GM since 1908, was dragged out the back and garrotted.

Ford Falcon EA

Tainted wagon

You may not recall the Falcon EA. But Ford Australia certainly does. It had to recall tens of thousands of them.

Ford Australia was defensive from the off. The word 'quality' was mentioned dozens of times at the launch, the factory-fitted rear-window stickers pushed the same line and, in retrospect, the brochure didst protest too much.

No amount of spruiking could change the reality: Ford Australia's Bicentennial Big Car, its first new Falcon in a decade, was a dog with fleas. Not that it was entirely a bad design. The EA had bodywork that was modern, sleek and rounded, yet still rugged enough to look the part as a taxi or police car. It was roomy and quick too, particularly when powered by the optional 3.9 L multipoint 'six'. But the Falcon EA came to market underdeveloped and the harm that its woeful build quality did to Falcon's reputation would linger for the rest of the century.

The EA range surfaced in early 1988, after a decade of the dependable but unexciting XE-XD-XF series. The launch generated plenty of excitement but soon there were recalls, bitchy articles and a large number of owners weighing in with their own none-too-complimentary thoughts. As if to support the case for the prosecution, the entire steering column of one newly minted EA dropped completely off its dashboard mountings and onto this writer's knees. Mid-corner.

It hadn't helped that Ford Australia was trying to bring the Capri roadster to market at roughly the same time as the new

Falcon. The struggling folk were also readying for market their version of the Nissan Pintara, called Corsair and just as ghastly. The Capri and Corsair both fronted late (in 1989), were equally doomed and, along with the cost of rectifying the EA debacle, helped raise serious doubts about the company's future as a manufacturer in Australia.

All things considered, it was an era the company would rather forget.

Pricing was another EA problem. The base model was $19,431, to which you had to add $460 if you wanted an auto (90 per cent of buyers did), plus all the other charges deceptively buried in the small print. In other words, the drive-away price of even the cheapest Falcon had exceeded $20,000 for the first time. And air-conditioning added yet another $1435.

Within a few months Holden had unboxed its new Commodore VN. This lacked the Falcon's surefooted stance and had its own quality problems, but it seemed a better value package and could at last match Ford for interior room. The VN enabled Holden to overhaul Falcon in the sales race for the first time since 1981 and – even more pleasingly for GM bean counters – the VN was cheaper to build and easier to update than the Falcon.

Late in 1989 the EA Series II Falcons were released with a lot of unseen but much-needed refinements. The next year brought '30th anniversary' upgrades, which was ironic. The first Falcon had been the 1960 XK and Ford Australia had been brought to the brink by the cost of rectifying problems with that model as well.

Ligier

It was built by one-time Formula One racing car constructor Ligier, but this little French box on wheels had only one motor sport connection: it was the pits.

Due to an almost inexplicable loophole in French road laws that existed until the early 1990s, a vehicle with an engine capacity of less than 125mL (or an output of less than 4 kW) did not need to be registered, nor did the person behind the wheel need to hold a driving licence.

This led to the development of a type of little car the French derisively referred to as a *pot du yaourt* (pot of yogurt). The *PdY* found immediate favour with very old and very young drivers, while rental companies bulk purchased them to offer to those whose licences had been suspended for drink-driving. Ligier was just one of several companies happy to supply.

Weaving in and out of manic Parisian traffic, these tubs of curdled milk were not governed by noise or pollution laws and their engines (usually two-stroke petrol engines, sometimes diesel and very occasionally electric) tended to spit out palls of dark smoke as they clackchuttered along. And, in accordance with French automotive custom, when *PdY*s were parked it was invariably on pedestrian crossings, across footpaths or on top of motorcyclists. Since they carried no registration plates or labels of identification, the owners couldn't be brought to account by police, though the vehicles themselves were often lifted and moved, or even capsized by aggrieved fellow citizens.

Despite tougher regulations (including the requirement that they be registered and wear number plates), the *PdY* still hasn't been completely stamped out.

VW Country Buggy

Sink, sank, sunk

There are many odd things about the VW Country Buggy. But nothing is odder than the fact it was designed to rescue a company that couldn't make money building the world's most successful car.

The story goes something like this: when the VW Beetle became an unexpected hit in Australia during the 1950s, local assembly commenced and plans were laid for a full-scale manufacturing operation in Clayton, Victoria.

Volkswagen Australasia Pty Ltd (VWA) was formed in 1957, the first sheet metal panels were produced in 1960 and by 1967 most Beetle mechanical components were also Australian-made. The only problem was that, as VWA's investment increased in pursuit of 95 per cent local content, Beetle sales fell in almost perfect unison. The bottom line required 50,000 cars a year. At no time during the 1960s did VWA come even close to achieving it.

As the local operation drowned in red ink, the Aussie Beetle was deprived of even the modest styling and mechanical updates fitted to German versions. More modern offerings, including the Mini Minor and a new breed of Japanese cars, grabbed an increasing share of the budget car market.

So what was the answer? VWA's director of quality control, Rudi Herzmer, thought it was a unique-to-Australia, 'go anywhere' vehicle loosely modeled on the German Army Kubelwagen, which he had worked on. This used standard Beetle mechanical components and was announced in February 1967. What's more, like the delightfully named Schwimmwagen variant of the World War II military vehicle, the Australian vehicle would be amphibious.

A press preview of the incredible floating VW – temporarily dubbed 'The Thing' – was held at Hume Weir, near Albury, New South Wales. Herzmer was seriously lobbying for the Kubelwagen name. Some journalists suggested instead that it was a blend of Jeep and Moke and should be called Joke.

The production version was released several months later, with the uninspiring handle of 'Country Buggy'. The base price had been set at $1550. The engine choice was between the 1.2 L and 1.3 L Dak-Dak units, while buyers could specify a four-speed manual gearbox . . . or a four-speed manual gearbox. Other options included buying the Country Buggy, and not buying it.

In this spirit, a printed summary issued to the press remarked that 'little consideration has been given to expensive and useless adornment.' Test-drivers were to soon find that little consideration had been given to many other aspects as well. The Country Buggy's motive power went strictly to the rear; the fact that the engine was directly over the drive wheels was supposedly enough to justify the 'go anywhere' tag. One place the production version of the new VeeDub wouldn't go, however, was across a pond. The amphibious capability had been quietly dropped following directives from the German factory. The crucial word here is quietly, because at least one unknowing journalist drove a Country Buggy down a boat ramp and sank.

Another place the Country Buggy refused to go was out a showroom door. Despite the addition of the incredible (non-floating) Country Buggy, VWA managed to sell just 11,000 vehicles of all varieties in 1968, including a mere 842 Country Buggies. The game was up. VWA dropped the Buggy, wrote off $20 million in plant and equipment and returned the Clayton plant to a simple assembly operation. The factory was eventually sold to Nissan, which managed to lose so much money building cars there (try $1 billion), that VW's problems seemed almost minor in comparison.

Jensen Interceptor

Going for broke

By the time the Jensen Interceptor appeared in 1966, the practice of cramming large American engines into English sports cars was already firmly established. And when it came to finding a large piece of US iron, Jensen – an English coach-building firm with a heritage going back to the 1920s – didn't muck about. It started with a 6.2 L Chrysler V8 and soon moved up to a 7.2 L version.

The Interceptor was handsome, luxuriously appointed and quick. The fastest version could touch 140 mph or 225 km/h. But promoting it from interesting to remarkable was the fact that a four-wheel drive version (known as the 'FF') was also produced. Using an innovative centre differential system developed by tractor magnate Harry Ferguson, the Interceptor FF was the world's first four-wheel drive high-performance car, and led to a whole new philosophy about how to get the most high-speed traction and performance.

Or to put it in more cynical terms, on-road four-wheel drive enabled owners to lose control at an even greater speed (in the same way that a good off-road four-wheel drive system allows people to become bogged in even more inaccessible places).

Four-wheel drive wasn't all that set the FF apart. The Interceptor FF (distinguished from the standard model by an extra vent or gill behind each front wheel) had Dunlop Maxaret anti-skid brakes, originally developed for jet planes. These two major innovations were described by Jensen as 'mechanical guardian angels'.

Visually, the most spectacular thing about the Interceptor (with a body penned by Italy's Touring studio) was the hatchback tail with its huge curved rear window. The Interceptor was shown at the Sydney Motor Show of 1969, with a price-tag of $16,900 for the two-wheel drive model and $20,000 for the FF. Both versions had a three-speed auto box (also from Chrysler) and four seats, although the two rear seats were not suitable for people with legs.

Despite its guardian angels, the FF version couldn't be saved. It was as dear as it was complicated (in both cases, far too) and production ceased with just 318 examples built. The rear-drive version continued but by the early 1970s a two-wheel drive Jensen Interceptor Series III cost around $23,000 in Australia. That made it markedly more expensive than a Porsche 911, BMW CS coupe or V12 Jaguar.

Like so many British cars, the Jensen suffered a litany of electrical woes, suspension problems and overheating (with resulting melting of under-bonnet hoses and wires). Its engine capacity guaranteed profligate fuel use.

The Interceptor convertible and coupe models (the latter a seemingly pointless 'fixed head' version of the former) were launched in 1974 and 1975 respectively, by which time Jensen was in receivership. It was a victim of a changing market, British industrial relations, the oil crisis, the cost of the Interceptor development and the disastrous Jensen-Healey project. In 1976 Jensen experienced the first of several closedowns, but in 1983 the company climbed back up onto its elbows and, amazingly, managed to crawl forward for another ten years before succumbing to the inevitable.

The final Series IV Interceptor was priced in the UK at £100,000, compared with the original price of £3742. At neither price, though, was it profitable.

Leyland Force 7

The death of Australia's Edsel, the Leyland P76, meant a variant that would have been the first modern-style, mass-produced Australian hatchback also bought the farm.

The Force 7 followed the early 1970s fashion of having a sports derivative of the everyday family sedan. Unfortunately, it was scheduled for 1974 release – the exact time Holden, Falcon and Valiant were preparing to phase out their coupes because the daft fad for large cars with enormous doors and small interiors had passed.

Leyland wasn't deterred. Its entry would be available in such colours as Oh Fudge and Home on th'Orange and, unlike the competing vehicles, had unique sheet-metal from nose to tail. Road testing soon revealed severe – some say fatal – structural rigidity problems. Nonetheless, about 60 Force 7s were sent down the line before Leyland hit the canvas. For reasons not entirely clear, all but ten were destroyed.

Chrysler Centura

The *other* French bomb

The formula seemed to work elsewhere: start with a European car, whack in as many Australian-made components as you can (but import all the really difficult bits) and reap the rewards.

Holden had the Torana, which had developed from the Vauxhall Viva, while Ford was increasingly cramming the Cortina with Falcon components to improve margins and meet local content requirements.

Chrysler, however, wasn't going down the English route. Why should it, when its acquisitive parent now owned a swag of continental brands? Bugger Bognor (or any other part of the Old Country), Chrysler Australia was going to market the Centura, a mid-size sedan with a distinctly Gallic flavour.

This, in retrospect, was not a good idea. The difficulties went beyond the 'near enough is much too close' ethos of French manufacturing during that era. The really big snag was a series of nuclear explosions set off in the Pacific by Georges Pompidou (who was a French president before he became a spectacularly ugly building).

When the first Centura shipments arrived from Simca in France in mid-1973, various Australian trade unions put a ban on handling the tainted objects. Chrysler Australia's plan had been to launch the car in late 1973, but some of these parts and panels were to gather rust for nearly two years before the Centura's eventual launch. By then several changes had been instituted, including upping the capacity of the imported four-cylinder engine from 1.8 L to 2.0 L and offering the Valiant's locally-built 4.0 L '245' Hemi six as the top engine.

This emphasis on cubic inches led to another problem. Chrysler expected to grab a healthy share of the four-cylinder market from Ford and Holden but buyers favoured the Centura six over the four by a huge margin. Many long-term Chrysler owners opted for a Centura 245 instead of a bigger, dearer (and more profitable) 'family-sized' Valiant. They did not seem deterred by the fact the big six gave the Centura, in the words of *Sun-Herald* road tester Evan Green, 'all the purpose and graceful balance of a bull in a trotting gig'.

At the most optimistic assessment, the Centura was roomy and handsome (in a bland sort of way). It also came with reasonable equipment levels. But it was cumbersome and thirsty, with a choppy ride, heavy steering and a price-tag generally considered to be much too high for a mid-sized car. The four-cylinder version was less nose-heavy but its dated engine made it significantly slower than the six without being significantly more economical. It was soon dropped from the line-up. Then there was the quality control, which was short on both quality and control. The New South Wales motorists' organisation, the NRMA, anonymously bought a Centura from a Sydney dealership for evaluation. Problems ranged from a cigarette lighter that didn't fit in its socket to major safety concerns such as wipers that didn't wipe and seatbelt retractors that didn't retract.

The NRMA reported that the fit and finish was dismal and leaks from within and without were rampant. After three weeks of warranty rectification, the NRMA's car was returned with several new problems, including front indicators that came on when the brakes were applied (even Alfa would be proud of that one!). Maybe it was all due to the use of parts that had been sitting around for so long, or maybe it was altogether a silly idea to Australianise and 'six-cylinderise' a French four-pot.

At the launch, Chrysler predicted it would produce 20,000 Centuras a year. It didn't come close. Production ground to an undignified halt after little more than 30 months.

Triumph Mayflower

More an Adversity than a Triumph, the Mayflower was a ludicrous attempt to graft the bodywork and associated grandeur of a large and powerful British limousine onto a small and powerless Triumph chassis.

Introduced in 1949, it acquired nicknames such as 'the watch charm Rolls-Royce', plus many things less kind. The vehicle and the opportunistic name were apparently created to appeal to Americans. It was assumed they held English limousines in high regard and therefore would go for the same thing in a concentrate.

Unfortunately, nobody asked the Americans what they thought before production commenced, and Triumph ended up shipping only a few more Mayflowers to the New World than the Pilgrims had in 1620. The company came to its senses in 1953 and abolished the model, then wrote it out of most official corporate histories.

Holden Camira

Gone with the wind

When the second fuel shock arrived at the end of the 1970s, Holden quickly moved to take disadvantage of the situation.

It did so by planning what would be one of its least fondly remembered cars, an absolute shocker that would never overcome the bad will it generated in its first year on the market.

The Camira – it's an Aboriginal word for 'soft wind' – was Holden's version of GM's new so-called World Car and was produced down-under from 1982. It was Holden's first front-drive local car, and for one short, shining moment the roominess of its interior and the good fuel economy of its 1.6 L 'four' made it seem the ideal thing for the times.

Wheels and *Modern Motor* magazines named Camira as the car of 1982, and Holden crowed while Ford Australia frantically started work on a 'me too' model. Many journalists predicted Australian motorists would abandon the traditional family six *en masse* in favour of this smaller, more frugal alternative.

They were right, too – up to a point. The punters did indeed arrive in a huge rush to buy the Camira, but they left in an even bigger hurry, turning the model into one of Holden's worst ever financial disasters.

The praise of many journalists had been inspired by the Camira's free-revving engine and excellent high-speed handling. But the ability to conquer off-camber sweepers in high gears with the tacho needle bouncing off the limiter created far less excitement among typical buyers. The mums and be-cardiganned dads who made up a large percentage of the Camira's early customers were more interested in why the thing was so badly put together, why every interior component rattled or squeaked, why there was so little low-down urge, and why it was necessary to keep taking the car back for warranty work. And when these owners looked at their fuel bills, they wondered if the savings justified having so much less room, power and rugged reliability than they were used to.

Aside from the woeful build quality, there was the issue of the Camira looking far too much like Holden's Commodore. The sales figures showed that almost every single person who purchased a Camira bought it instead of its dearer (and considerably more profitable) big brother. Falcon sales did dip slightly during the fuel crisis, but Holden had a much worse problem. It was saddled with the cost of building two different car-lines for almost exactly the same number of sales it could have achieved with one. As a final kick in the guts, there was a fuel glut on the way.

Holden stylists were soon given the job of making the Commodore look bigger and the Camira smaller, while Ford quietly dropped its own plans for a direct Camira competitor.

A better-built and more refined 'JD' Camira was launched with a more torquey 1.8 L engine, and a further improved 2.0 L 'JE' followed. Holden had once boasted the Camira would become Australia's best-selling car. Sales fell to as low as 10,000 a year and, when replacement time came, the company closed the line, killed the name and stuck 'Holden Apollo' badges on a little changed Toyota Camry.

AMC Pacer

Marketing textbooks define durable goods as consumer products that are typically used over an extended period and can survive repeated uses. The AMC Pacer was neither durable nor good.

What American Motors Corp. (AMC) called 'the first wide small car' appeared in mid-1975 and was grossly overweight, surprisingly tight on elbow room (despite a considerable girth), prone to cooking its occupants under that huge glasshouse, and diabolical in the handling stakes. Other than that, there weren't too many problems, except, of course, that it was shoddily screwed together and ugly. Really, really ugly. And if googly eyes and a ridiculously bulbous tail with a huge overhang over the side of each rear wheel weren't enough, the Pacer was expensive to build and buy and, despite its so-called subcompact dimensions, it guzzled fuel.

The short bonnet was originally shaped for a GM-built Wankel engine. When this was stillborn, AMC engineers instead jammed in their hefty and well-aged six, making the Pacer as agile as an ocean liner and as desirable as gout.

Purvis Eureka

Flat, strapped

Since the dawn of the motor era, men have tried to perpetuate their name by having it on the badge of a car. One such man was Allan C. Purvis, who claimed in the late 1980s that his eponymous company was Australia's seventh biggest car-maker.

With a background in advertising and industrial design, Purvis was among hundreds or even thousands of Australians who dreamt of running his (and very occasionally, her) own car company. Purvis made it further than most, building about 650 kit cars between 1974 and 1988. It was never easy, however, and almost certainly never profitable. Purvis Cars Pty Ltd had to overcome a fire, which in 1979 destroyed almost everything, and endlessly battled to keep the show on the road in the face of constant financial challenges. One bizarre proposal to reduce production costs involved inmates at Sydney's Long Bay jail building Eurekas as part of a rehabilitation program.

Purvis had set up shop in Victoria in 1974, planning to make an 'Australianised' version of the Nova fibreglass-bodied sports car. Designed in England and influenced by such vehicles as the Ford GT40, this was almost a cartoon parody of a 1970s sports car, so low and pointy it didn't look quite real. The same vehicle was built in the USA as the Sterling and had various other names in other countries.

Behind the extreme appearance was a garden variety VW Beetle platform and Dak-Dak mechanical components. A favourable response at the 1974 Melbourne Motor Show encouraged Purvis to offer a do-it-yourself version plus a full 'turn-key', or ready to drive away, model. Among the claims were that the newcomer was an 'economy sports car', more aerodynamically efficient and 20 per cent lighter than a standard Beetle, and thus capable of delivering better performance and economy.

The Eureka's overall height was 1.067 metres: low enough to trip over. But the most novel (and for some, worrying) aspect of the Eureka was the large lift-up roof section, through which the driver and passenger entered and exited. This was raised manually, though an electrically-powered mechanism – with a reputation for trapping people inside and out – was also available. Other areas of the Purvis were equally crude. However, if you did all the work yourself you could get a Eureka onto the road for a fraction the price of anything else that looked anywhere near as exotic.

A *Wheels* magazine road test concluded: 'To own a Purvis Eureka you'd have to be prepared to tolerate claustrophobic accommodation, a noisy body, poor wet weather vision and a thousand and one niggling faults that would be intolerable on any production car. Against this would have to be weighed the pride of ownership or the pose value.'

For most people, pride and pose didn't provide a big enough trade-off. Sales in the 1980s were lean, to say the least. The knockout blow, according to Purvis, was the failure to secure a federal government research and development grant for a convertible version of the Eureka, known as the Free Spirit. The 'For Sale' sign went up in 1988 and the company changed hands a couple more times before the Eureka largely faded away.

The final Purvis tally was 650 sold, 450 registered. The discrepancy, one suspects, was due to a couple of hundred enthusiasts setting off on the dream and tripping along the frustrating path. Allan Purvis, and countless other would-be car magnates, would have known exactly how they felt.

Panther Rio

The first Panthers were retro-cars inspired by pre-war Jaguars and Bugattis. In 1975, however, the company changed tack with the truly bizarre Rio, aimed at Rolls-Royce buyers who needed something more economical.

On the plus side of the ledger, the Rio was half the price of the vehicle it aspired to be. On the debit, it was three times the price of the car it really was: a Triumph Dolomite. Why anybody would base anything on a Triumph Dolomite was a question almost too scary to ask.

There was a hand-beaten aluminium outer skin, leather and walnut inside and little Union Jacks on the door sills. But there was also the Dolomite's harsh gear-change, heavy clutch and iffy reliability. Actually, there was nothing iffy about the Dolomite. It was sure to break down.

Just 38 Rios were built. Or, to put it another way: despite everything you've just read, as many as 38 Rios were built.

Ford Landau

Coupe de vile

The late 1960s and early 1970s saw many bold attempts by Australian car-makers to reinvent their everyday family sedans as luxury saloons. Ford had the most success with its Fairlane series; Chrysler the least with its naffly-named 'Chrysler by Chrysler'.

Even less successful than the 'Chrysler by Chrysler' saloon, however, was the same model's two-door variant. The Chrysler Hardtop left the people energetically shouting for less, and how Ford later found itself in the same ditch with the Landau is hard to imagine.

Some Ford sources said the US Thunderbird was the inspiration for the Landau Hardtop, but that sounds like after-the-fact rationalisation. In fact, Ford was trying to get a bit more value out of a new – and grotesque – front-end it had created for a different model called the LTD.

The LTD was the result of Ford Australia's decision to further stretch the Fairlane, an already stretched (perhaps overly so) version of the Falcon. For years the company had been locally assembling the giant US-built Galaxie LTD, but this was becoming too expensive and a local replacement was needed.

It came when the Aussie LTD – spruiked as 'the most luxurious car ever built in Australia' – was launched in 1973. Despite the Chrysler Hardtop's earlier failure, Ford went ahead and produced the two-door Landau as a companion to the LTD. The stablemates were presented as 'Australia's most distinguished motorcars'.

80 • EXTRA LEMON!

This was a meaningless expression only outdone for meaninglessness by the 'personal coupe' term that Ford applied to the Landau (unless it referred to the fact that rear leg room was almost nil despite the large exterior dimensions, or to the selfishness of driving such a large car during the early 1970s fuel crisis).

Like the LTD, the Landau used mainly Falcon mechanical components and was crammed with almost every accessory Ford had access to. It featured a 5.8 L V8 engine as standard equipment, plus electric windows (operated by those long, round-headed ultra-1970s chrome buttons), air-conditioning, automatic transmission, press-button radio, huge domed wheel trims and the novelty of concealed-headlamps set flush into a wide and weighty grille. Perhaps the most notable inclusion was four-wheel disc brakes, a first for a mainstream Australian car.

The body of the Landau comprised the LTD's front panels with the Falcon Hardtop's rear. The side-window openings were slightly revised, however, to give a more stately appearance and justify a $6950 price tag. Also included, in the hope of justifying such a huge ask for the era, were a fake-timber instrument panel, ultra-plush seat trim, a carpeted boot and a padded vinyl roof (which also provided a useful way of covering the joins of the crudely modified side window openings).

The fuel crisis wasn't the Landau's only problem. The market's appetite for big two-doors was diminishing even before it was launched and this trend would soon spell the end of the Valiant Charger and Holden Monaro models, as well as the Falcon Hardtop and its Landau offspring.

The afterthought nature of Ford's big two-door luxo-barge also worked against it. The vacuum-operated headlight hoods were unreliable and expensive to repair, the electrical system was problematic, the tarty trim deteriorated quickly and the body was susceptible to rust, particularly under that stupid vinyl roof. In early 1976 – less than three years after its launch – the Landau disappeared from new car price lists. In its last days it had carried a sticker of $11,000 but you could almost halve its value by driving it out of the car yard.

Panther 6

More is less

It was in England in 1972 that Panther Westwinds Ltd commenced business – if selling cars at a financial loss can be called a business. As well as blending a Rolls-Royce and Triumph Dolomite in its strange and unnecessary Rio model, Panther made an even odder contribution to the motoring world of the 1970s.

It was a sports machine known as the 6, on account of it having 50 per cent more wheels than most people expected when they bought a car. The idea of a six-wheeled road car wasn't entirely new. A few cross-country vehicles had been built with an extra set of wheels, just in case. But the Panther was certainly the first sports car thus equipped, with its extra wheels said to be there for improved on-road acceleration, braking and handling.

The downside of the unusual layout was that it cost more and nobody really needed it. But that seemed a small consideration when you saw how much press was generated by the announcement of this vehicle.

The idea was already proven, up to a point, by the Tyrrell racing team, which had won a Grand Prix the previous year with a six-wheeled Formula One car. Tyrrell used conventional wheels at the rear, but tiny wheels on the front, reducing the height – and therefore the aerodynamic drag – of the front end. In the process it also put more rubber on the road for greater cornering grip.

The Panther 6 of 1977, however, used almost the same sized wheels on the front as the back, capturing many of the disadvantages of having six-wheels (extra weight, complexity and rolling resistance), without a profile that afforded a really low ground-hugging nose. And to house a 7.9 L Cadillac V8 with twin turbochargers, the Panther 6 had the longest tail in the automotive kingdom.

Between the long nose and even longer tail was a tiny two-seater cockpit, nestled behind a vast windscreen. The instruments were digital, there was a television and phone, plenty of leather and suede, and very little elbow room.

The overall styling treatment brought to mind Lady Penelope's car in the original *Thunderbirds* television series. The quoted price was a then-monstrous £40,000, but it was said that 15 orders were taken at the British Motor Fair of 1977. A year later, company owner Robert Jankel (pictured on previous page) seemed no closer to fulfilling orders for the Panther 6, so he organised for some motoring magazines to have supervised access to the car, presumably in the hope this would convince the doubters. Jankel first explained to the road testers that the production delays were solely due to Pirelli not supplying the right tyres, so some special allowances had to be made for the handling idiosyncrasies.

Under the heading 'Is it a bird? Is it a plane? Is it a joke?', the UK's *Motor* magazine took to the wheel and – having identified various unusual handling tendencies in a straight line – threw it into a corner. 'Certainly the sheer adhesion of all that rubber is tremendous, but at high cornering speeds you are very much aware of the huge mass of engine behind you, threatening to swing the tail out like a massive pendulum.'

The magazine also found the steering non-communicative, the brakes lacking, a tendency for the front tyres to 'tramline' and the acceleration from rest less than expected of such an enormous engine. Yet the journalist still walked away seemingly of the opinion that some new tyres and a bit of carburettor tuning would calm the savage beast. 'There is some fine honing to be done [but] it works, it's for real, and it's beautifully made,' was the remarkably soft conclusion. Panther never had the chance to prove the case. Series production never eventuated, supposedly because of the problem with obtaining tyres. Rather than buyers. By 1980 the company was in receivership.

Ssangyong Korando

There were many stupid things about the Korando, but perhaps the most dippy was the name. Korando isn't a majestic beast, a celestial body, an egotistical automotive magnate or any of the other things people usually name cars after. It's a corruption of 'Korea can do'. And that's despite the fact that one look at this crimped-nose Jeep makes it immediately obvious that if there is one thing Korea can do, it's not this.

English designer Ken Greenley penned the lines and argued they would make people stand up and take notice, thereby helping establish Ssangyong as a distinct and successful brand.

So did the strategy work? Shortly after the model's launch, the company was absorbed into Daewoo, which soon collapsed three-quarters dead into the arms of General Motors. In a word, no.

Suzuki X90

Coming, ready or not

'You've never driven anything like this before!' announced the Suzuki X90 brochure, and for once a brochure was accurate. The conveyance in question was squat and unsightly, daft in concept and lousy in packaging. And it rode like a boneshaker bicycle.

The X90 had originally been shown in concept form at the Tokyo Motor Show, supposedly to test public reaction. The public reacted, but Suzuki proceeded anyway.

The first X90s hit Australian shores in 1996 and Suzuki boasted the newcomer represented a 'triumph in pure visual appeal'. A vehicle responsible for such a remarkable accomplishment in aesthetics might have been expected to command a premium in the market. However, the X90 was introduced at a relatively modest $23,990 and this price was cut by $1000 three months later and by a further $2000 in early 1997.

The X90 might have succeeded if it had looked fan-bloody-tastic. Punters have shown again and again that they are prepared to buy something on looks, despite all other considerations. But by mid-1997, the X90 was selling for just $17,990. Or, to be more precise, it was failing to sell at $17,990. Dealers would have had an easier time clearing diplodocus evacuations from their showroom floors.

The mechanical components were for the most part borrowed from the Suzuki Vitara stablemate, with a 1.6 L four-cylinder engine, four-wheel drive and a choice between five-speed manual and four-speed auto transmissions. A dual ratio 4WD set-up was provided, though the reason for this was not given.

The brochure boasted of such safety features as 'three-point seatbelts, side impact protection, head restraints', all of which were the bare minimum required by law. By the same logic, luxury equipment included doors, seats and a steering wheel.

'In the Xtreme' was the slogan, a reference perhaps to a body with the packaging efficiency of a roadster, whacked on top of a drivetrain that ensured the high centre of gravity, rotten dynamics and questionable on-road safety of an all-terrain vehicle. Another problem was the vehicle's strictly two-seater nature, coupled with a small boot further cramped by a poorly placed spare wheel and bulky pockets for housing the T-Top roof panels.

The Sydney Morning Herald called the X90 a 'misguided attempt to attract the youth vote'. That youth wasn't going to tick the box, donkey style, was shown by the fact that by late 1997 Suzuki's Australian operation was still trying to clear the 484 cars it had imported during 1996.

No 1997 models were brought in and the final three X90s (still 1996 compliance) were finally inflicted on customers in 1999. Suzuki muttered something about the concept being ahead of its time. Yeah, right.

Sabra Sports

It was going to be Israel's big automotive break. It was going to be a dashing two-seater roadster made in Haifa. It was going to be exported to the US in big numbers. As it turned out, it wasn't, it wasn't and it wasn't.

The company behind the project – Autocars Co. Ltd – had already achieved modest success building versions of British Reliant three- and four-wheelers for the Israeli market and had even garnered some US interest when it displayed vehicles at the 1960 New York Trade Fair.

With his appetite for US action whetted, the company's managing director, Itzhak Shubinksy, spotted a vehicle he thought gave the best possible chance of making an impact. It was the UK-built, fibreglass-bodied Ashley GT, and Shubinksy snapped up the rights, renamed it after a cactus, and contracted Reliant to hurriedly re-engineer it for the US. Unfortunately, in the rush Reliant misheard Shubinksy and horridly re-engineered it.

Furthermore, the Autocars factory wasn't ready, so the Sabra Sports was made in the UK by Reliant and shipped directly to the US. Despite all the fuss, the plastic-bodied car with the strangely squared rear wheel-arches (and even stranger front bumper overriders), sold just 150 units in America and within a remarkably short time the Sabra Sports was cactus. Reliant tried to salvage some of its investment by launching the car in the UK as the Sabre, while Autocars went back to the boring utilitarian models that were its normal fare.

Tucker 48

Damned torpedo

The Tucker appears in some lists of the Greatest Cars Ever Built, and the man behind this late 1940s streamliner – Michigan-born former car salesman Preston Thomas Tucker – is the subject of a idolatrous film directed by Francis Ford Coppola.

The true believers will tell you Mr T was visionary, his car revolutionary, the whole venture a noble attempt to break Detroit's thoroughly evil GM-Ford-Chrysler cartel. This retelling suggests the Tucker car was festooned with technological and safety features that major makers had conspired to suppress, and that even the government was in on the plot to bring the upstart company down. In this David v. Goliath battle, Goliath was not only bigger, he was the one with the slingshot.

The case for the prosecution paints Preston Tucker as a shonk who wasted and even misappropriated most of the millions he raised from mum-and-dad investors. His project, they argue, was so fanciful the Big Three would not have lost even a moment's sleep over it, let alone hatched a major plot.

The story started in 1946 when Preston Tucker unveiled a sketch of his 'Torpedo', and produced a lot of fast talk about how this was a 'car of the future for the everyday man', and had already been the subject of 15 years of development. It was a good time to sell a dream; with the war over and a scarcity of new cars even from the major car-makers, there was plenty of pent-up demand and blue-sky optimism. Investors and potential dealers lined up to throw their money – a remarkable $26 million of it – at this tall and charming man in a sharp suit. Tucker also persuaded the War Assets Administration to do him a winning deal on a massive factory in Chicago.

The Torpedo prototype, now called the Tucker 48, was unveiled amid great showmanship in July 1947. However, beneath the glitz and gloss, the prototype was a hurriedly thrown together effort to placate increasingly nervous investors and the Securities and Exchange Commission (SEC), which had begun taking a keen interest in Tucker's business manoeuvres.

Designer Alex Tremulis drew up the body, based on Tucker's instructions, and produced something that looked slightly ahead of Detroit's mainstream efforts, but was hardly the leap into the distant future promised by the early sketches. One notable feature was a centre headlight that turned with the wheels.

Despite Tucker's claims of 'the first completely new car in 50 years', the transmission was salvaged from a prewar Cord and the prototype fabricated around a 1942 year model Oldsmobile body. The SEC would soon argue the Tucker operation had neither the expertise nor the serious intention to turn this hand-built one-off into a series production car.

The prototype also lacked many of the safety features Tucker had earlier boasted about (such as disc brakes and seatbelts). Of those that were present, the so-called crash padding on the dash was of dubious value and the provision of an area into which the front seat passenger could duck during a collision was just plain silly.

As for the mechanical layout, what worked for the VW Beetle was the stuff of comedy when what you hung over the back axle was a huge 'six' with a capacity of 589 ci, or 9.65 L. This massively heavy but not overly powerful engine needed two truck batteries to turn it over. If such a tail-heavy machine wasn't going to go around corners very happily – even with the smaller 335 ci (or 5.5 L) donk that replaced the original '589' – the Tucker should at least have been good in a straight line. The later engine was designed for a helicopter and supposedly produced 165 bhp (123 kW), compared with the Chevy six's 90 bhp (67 kW). On the other hand, the Tucker weighed more than 2 tonnes and the power output figures were as suspect as Tucker's claimed '130 mph top speed' and '35 miles per gallon' fuel economy.

A pilot production run of 50 cars was pushed through to convince investors and the SEC, which had stepped up its investigations when Mr T raised yet more money with an advance purchase plan on Tucker 48 accessories. These 50 cars were hand-built at monumental expense, yet the price was a bargain $2450.

In 1948 Tucker published an open letter outlining his woes. His factory, he wrote, was infiltrated with industrial spies and he was being undermined by competitors with friends 'in high places in Washington'. He suggested elsewhere that other carmakers were bullying their suppliers into withholding parts. Yet in reality, Tucker was years away from being in a position to order parts in serious quantities. It is also likely that Tucker's advertised price would send him broke at least as quickly as any skulduggery from competitors.

Tucker and his associates went to trial on 31 fraud charges but were eventually found not guilty. It was little consolation, because by then the Tucker concern was thoroughly bankrupt. In 1951 the man at the centre of it all did what any man in his circumstances would – he flew to Brazil to seek finance for another new car, this time a sports model called Carioca. This project still hadn't come to fruition when Tucker died of cancer in 1956, aged 53.

Ford Gyron

In 1961 Ford engineers announced they had cleverly used a gyroscope to stabilise a two-wheeled car. But they forgot to tell us why. The advantages of compactness that might – just might – be realised with such an unusual arrangement were completely lost in the ridiculous bodywork. The 'delta-shaped' Gyron was a limousine-like 5.3 metres (209 inches) in length, and more than 2 metres wide. Yet it transported just two people.

Ford's head stylist called the Gyron 'an outstanding example of the visioneering that is the heart of progressive automotive styling'. All these years later, it still isn't known what the hell he was talking about.

The overall design concept, according to more gobbledygook from the styling team, was to break the link between the car and the carriage that preceded it; to use a starting point other than a square machine with a wheel at each corner. Features included a steering dial with separate inner rings to control the speed and direction of travel. This apparently allowed the vehicle to be driven from either seat.

And did the Ford move in mysterious ways? Er, no. The small print in the press release said 'Although the car is not operable in its present form, Ford stylists have been assured that a gyroscope no larger than two feet in diameter would be sufficient to stabilize the vehicle on its two wheels set in tandem'.

Even then, the Gyron required two small outrigger wheels at the rear to stabilise it while the gyroscope built up enough revs. Daft? You bet.

Ilinga AF2

Local sports, take 52

Forget previous attempts to launch an all-Aussie sports car, this is the real thing. At last, here is a car project with the budget, the styling, the technology and the marketing nous to be nothing short of an Australian Ferrari.

If this 1975 pitch sounds familiar, it's because the Ilinga AF2 was but one in a long line of heavily spruiked Great Slight Hopes. And like the vast majority of its forebears and descendants, the Ilinga was knocked to the canvas almost before the bell had announced the first round.

That's not to say the Ilinga deserved to be king-hit; the two-door, four-seater was ambitious in concept, impressive in execution and generally a better than average contender. There were some heart problems, though, which we'll come to shortly.

The first example was wheeled out in February 1975 and there was no shortage of confidence. The managing director of Ilinga Pty Ltd, Daryl Davies, told *The National Times* it was the safest car on the market. The brochure compared the launch of Ilinga with the birth of Mercedes, Alfa Romeo and Jaguar: 'In years to come you will be able to say you were there when the legend of Ilinga was born.' Unfortunately most people will now reply, 'What was Ilinga?', but back in 1975 there was an unusually enthusiastic response from the public and press.

The V8-powered coupe had a claimed top speed of 200 km/h. The plan was to manufacture 100 units a year for sale at $15,750 apiece. That was more than three times the price of a Holden sedan, but still $4000 cheaper than a Porsche 911.

Over $200,000 had been spent on Ilinga development, it was boasted. But the specification sheet revealed a major problem:

the 'heart' was the 4.4 L Leyland P76 engine. Such a choice might well have made a small amount of sense when Ilinga development started in 1973 (a very small amount), but by 1975 Leyland had ceased P76 production.

The Ilinga's well-finished body sat on a box section chassis, while aluminium panels were used to save weight. The 'safety cell' body supposedly ensured the engine would slide under the passenger compartment in the event of a collision. To save cost, the Ilinga had a front-mounted engine with live rear axle and made do with many familiar parts including Volvo bumpers. However, in other departments it did not skimp on luxury or mechanical equipment, boasting air-conditioning, Recaro sports seats, ventilated disc brakes, concealed headlights, a stereo radio/cassette and a central door-locking system that could automatically close the electric windows and extinguish the lights. There was even a folding umbrella that slid into a special compartment within the driver's door.

The automatic transmission, however, became the subject of a major kerfuffle. Ilinga directors claimed that, despite promises and contracts, the transmission delivered by Borg-Warner would not successfully mate with the P76 V8. It was this, rather than a question mark over engine supply, which was jeopardising the venture, they announced, adding that the little Ilinga company was prepared to take on the might of Borg-Warner in the courts. As it turned out, the court case didn't proceed and neither did Ilinga. A second example was built but at this point the Ilinga – its name an Aboriginal expression for 'far horizon' – rode off into the sunset.

Daihatsu Bee

In the early 1950s Daihatsu attempted to make a passenger car out of one of its three-wheeled delivery trucks. The result – which finally came to market in 1958 after several false starts – had a side profile that looked like a conventional saloon car in the hope no-one would notice it was missing a front wheel. To further confuse the enemy, it had a long bonnet, despite the engine being in the tail.

Even when its styling was put to one side, where it belonged, the Bee was not the knees. It was crude in construction, woefully underpowered (production versions had a dubious 540 cc air-cooled engine that struggled to drag along the new bodywork) and not altogether stable. Sales were infinitesimal. It was a decade or so before the company built its first four-wheeled passenger car and many more years further on before it produced anything you'd feel even slightly safe sitting in.

Holden Brougham

Stringing out the tail

Holden had the local car market of the 1950s largely to itself, but it was Ford Australia and its Falcon that was the big mover of the 1960s. After a slow start, Henry beat The General to market with such options as an auto trannie, disc brakes and a V8 engine. Falcon was also first to market with a two-door coupe and a serious high-performance variant (the GT Falcon).

But the real masterstroke, in accounting terms if no other, was the idea of building a Fairlane luxury car on the Falcon's extended wagon platform. This type of car could fetch a huge premium in the showroom, yet, thanks to sharing much of its body structure and almost all its mechanical equipment with the cheaper Falcon, would cost only a small amount more to build.

When the Aussie-made Fairlane hit the market in 1967, it

bridged the price gap between the local cars and the luxury imports and gave buyers unbeatable metal for the money. It also sent Holden into such a tizz that it would be more than two decades before it came up with a satisfactory response.

All GM's early attempts were dismal, but none was worse than the first, which produced the vile Brougham. Rushed to market in 1968, this was such a quick fix there was no time to stretch the wheelbase. The brochure said the styling was incomparable. It was, but not in a positive way because Holden had created its lengthened luxury car by taking the HK Premier and stretching the boot.

With an extra 200 mm of sheet metal behind the rear wheels, the word ungainly came to mind, though not quite as quickly as the words cheap and cynical. 'Australia's finest car' was the not-at-all-convincing slogan. Brochure writers tagged the newcomer 'a near-perfect blend of prestige, luxury, comfort, performance and safety' and 'noticeably longer, dramatically more beautiful than any Holden before it'. Worst of all, because the front end looked the same as the Premier's, the publicity photos had to concentrate on the preposterous tail.

By way of compensation, the Brougham was crammed with gimmicks, including a new type of 'island' vinyl roof, which didn't run all the way to the drainage rails, and a 'contrasting coach line hand-painted along each side'. Beat that, Ford!

Inside, there was thick carpet everywhere, even throughout the gigantic boot. Every interior surface that didn't have bona fide plastic wood stuck to it was padded and/or covered with 'imported brocade' upholstery, made of genuine vinyl. The armrest, doors and seats featured an elaborate Brougham emblem. Power came from the Chevrolet '307' V8 via an auto with just two speeds. And in keeping with those more spartan times, this perfect blend of luxury and comfort listed air-conditioning, power windows and transistor radio as expensive options.

By the late 1960s Holden was working on a true long-wheelbase sedan, but it needed to update the Brougham two more times before this would be ready. The first revamp (the HT) introduced the Aussie-built 308 V8 engine, the next (the HG) featured a new three-speed auto gearbox called the Trimatic, but soon better known as the Traumatic. There was an all-new Brougham motif too, appropriately incorporating a wreath.

The Brougham's funeral was in mid-1971 and the job of being comprehensively thrashed by the Ford Fairlane was bequeathed to the new long-wheelbase HQ Statesman.

Moskvich

This is a wagon version of the Moskvich, a Russian sedan that owed its popularity entirely to there being almost no competition.

The Soviet government's Tass news agency – which also got by without a lot of competition – described the five-door variant as an exciting highlight of the Technica-Aesthetics-Progress Exhibition held in the Standards Pavilion at the USSR Economic Achievements Exhibition of 1970. Certainly the observers captured here are nearly beside themselves with excitement.

At around the same time, there was an attempt made to sell the Moskvich sedan in Australia. It lost just a little of its momentum when the evaluation model was loaned to Sydney motoring journalist Pedr Davis for a second opinion. On the first morning it refused to start. The following night it spontaneously combusted in his suburban driveway. Davis gave the potential importer a second opinion, and found time to offer a third and fourth as well.

Tass said the wagon's clever design allowed the rear seat to be folded 'within five minutes'. It also stressed the newcomer was attractive and safe, *attractive* and *safe* presumably being the Russian words for unsightly and exceedingly dangerous.

Toyota 2000GT

It only lived once

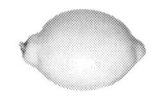

The US Stock Exchange is located in Broad Street, not Wall Street. Russia's October Revolution took place in November and the Hundred Years War was about 1.15 centuries long. Equally odd – and of more relevance to this story – is that the most famous Toyota of the 1960s started out as a joint project between Nissan and Yamaha.

That car, the 2000GT, is perhaps best known as the transport of James Bond's Japanese side-kick, Aki, in the film *You Only Live Twice*. Yet it was a sales disaster. One problem was the high price, another the fact that the wealthy Western buyers who were being targeted were not prepared to accept that the Japanese – only just starting to win grudging praise for their small and cheap runabouts – had any business being in the upmarket sports car field.

The 2000GT was sold only as a coupe, the convertible having been produced for the film. The tintop was light (a fraction over a tonne), low (1.13 metres) and spectacularly styled with its curved roof and sweeping fastback. Front-engined and rear drive, the 2000GT had a Lotus Elan-style backbone chassis and, also in the Lotus style, coil-sprung double-wishbone suspension all-round. It was the first Japanese production car to feature four-wheel disc brakes. The interior was crafted in the 1960s sports car tradition, with a wood-rimmed steering wheel, stubby gear-lever, perforated seating material and an extravagant plethora of dials, buttons and gauges, some of which possibly did nothing at all.

The exterior also demonstrated many stylistic hallmarks of the era: wire wheels, pop-up headlights and lots of air-ducts. The comparison most often made was with the E-Type Jaguar, though Toyota vigorously denied that the big cat had been its inspiration.

The developmental history of the car is a little hazy. Toyota claimed at the time it was totally designed and engineered by their good selves and that whereas, yes, the Yamaha company had been involved, that was only for assembly. Nissan (which withdrew from the project just before production began) was completely airbrushed out of the photo. Toyota ordered a few further changes to the original specifications of the vehicle, including the development of a twin cam head for what had started life as a Datsun/Prince Skyline straight six. The hybrid 2.0 L six – for which

Yamaha had done most of the work – used double overhead camshafts and was fed by three dual throat Mikuni-Solex carburettors to produce around 112 kW at 7000 rpm. It was described as being 'based on a Toyota engine', a statement falling somewhere between a terminological inexactitude and an outright falsehood.

The 2000GT was unveiled in prototype form at the 1965 Tokyo Motor Show, and went into production in 1966. The handful of 2000GTs that came to Australia in 1967 sold for around $5500. Or would have sold for $5500 if anyone was prepared to pay it. That was about two and a half times as much as a Holden sedan, and an unprecedented price for a Japanese car. Then again, the claimed top speed of 137 mph (221 km/h) was equally unprecedented for any four-wheeler stamped 'Made in Japan'. Even at that elevated price, Toyota couldn't make money.

The total production was about 330, including the two convertibles built for the Bond film. One of the ragtops – albeit an undriveable mock-up – came to Australia for the 1967 Sydney Motor Show. A sales lemon it might have been, but the 2000GT proved good news for those who hung on to original examples. What couldn't be sold for $5500 all those years ago will now fetch $150,000 and more.

Ford Pinto

Passengers alight here

The Pinto 'subcompact' was named after a horse. A piebald horse. A piebald horse with a tendency, one assumes, to explode.

The Ford that would become known as 'the barbeque that seats four' was rushed to market for the 1971 model year as a counter to Chevrolet's equally unexciting but considerable less flammable Vega. At first only a two-door Pinto sedan was offered, but the range was soon expanded to include a Runabout model with a hatch door at the rear, possibly to give easier access for rescue crews.

There was nothing innovative about the Pinto's styling or engineering, but the price was right, the four-cylinder engine was reasonably economical and sales were strong. But by 1974 Ralph

Nader's Center for Auto Safety was demanding a recall, arguing that the Pinto's tendency to concertina in rear-end accidents did more than rip open the badly positioned fuel tank. It also tended to jam the doors shut.

As combinations go, this was a rather worrying one, but Ford refused to change a thing, offering the Department of Transportation such inventive arguments as 'retooling for the changes would take 43 months' (considerably longer than it had taken to develop the entire car) and – wait for it – 'most of those people were already dead from the impact before the fire started'. By 1977, however, the growing band of Pintonista rebels had their manifesto. It was a brilliant piece of investigative journalism by Mark Dowie in *Mother Jones*, the curiously named magazine of the Foundation for National Progress.

Using internal Ford documents and hundreds of collision reports, this article (now archived on motherjones.com) detailed how Ford had conducted its own crash tests and was aware of the hazards awaiting those early buyers. Yet, Dowie wrote, Ford refused to modify the Pinto and even rejected as too dear a $1 plastic shield that significantly reduced chances of the exposed fuel tank being punctured. Ford had a design brief that demanded the car weigh 'not an ounce over 2000 pounds nor cost a cent over $2000' and was grimly sticking to it.

Dowie wrote that despite as many as 900 deaths in Pinto fires, Henry Ford II continued to vigorously campaign against new safety legislation. 'Compliance to these standards will shut down the industry,' Ford said, repeatedly. But what made the most impact was *Mother Jones*'s detailing of Ford's now-notorious 'cost-benefit analysis'. This assigned a value to each fatality of $200,000 and to each serious burning of $67,000 and argued that the cost of fixing the Pinto exceeded the cost of deaths and maimings (when calculated in such a way).

Ford's reluctance to modify was perhaps driven by arrogance, but also by the high cost of new tooling and the fact a different fuel tank would compromise boot space (an important selling feature). The Pinto continued to ignite debate – and motorists – and Ford even launched a 'woody wagon' version. Sure, its sides were covered with plastic woodgrain rather than real timber, but it still seemed to be adding fuel to the fire.

Ford said the *Mother Jones* article was filled with 'distortions and half truths', but it still recalled 1.5 million Pintos. Shortly after the recall started, however, these cost-benefit analysis calculations were blown to bits when a Californian jury awarded Pinto victim Richard Grimshaw a record US$125 million in punitive damages. A year later Indiana prosecutors charged Ford Motor Company executives with reckless homicide.

The Pinto's own funeral pyre was lit in 1980. The Grimshaw judgment was later reduced on appeal (to $3.5 million), the executives were acquitted on the reckless homicide charges and, strangely, none of the fuss had ever greatly hurt Pinto sales. So perhaps Ford was right all along: a low purchase price and a boot that takes a second set of golf clubs *is* better than a long life and happy retirement.

Nash Metropolitan

Cold comfort

No vehicle in history has managed as convincing an impersonation of a prostrate refrigerator on caster wheels. Perhaps then, it's no surprise that the Nash Metropolitan came from the corporation that also built Kelvinator whitegoods.

The Metropolitan would later become a collectable due to its Toyland appearance, but it completely failed to be popular in its day. This was despite intensive market research that appeared to show that such a car was just what American motorists of the 1950s were waiting for.

In many people's minds it was all Austin's fault. This is grossly unfair. Yes, the Austin Motor Company did build the Metropolitan, and it did so at its Longbridge plant in England. But it built the car entirely under contract, and to a US template. The styling was the work of independent designer William Flajole who – and I'm guessing here – hoped people would take the Metropolitan home because they felt sorry for it.

It was a lack of expertise in the small car field, and of the right production facilities, that led to the Nash-Kelvinator group outsourcing the manufacturing to the company considered the international leader in small cars at that time. And so, from early 1954, this most un-American of American vehicles arrived on US shores directly from Austin. A two-door hardtop and a convertible were offered. Both were short, narrow and top-heavy, with only a hint of wheel-arches and a strange notch in each door which, taking into account the refrigerator heritage, might have been modelled on a diary compartment.

The Metropolitan was highly specified, but not particularly cheap, despite its modest size and the fact the British pound was then as respected as British dentistry. The body was of a monocoque or unitary construction type. The spare tyre was on the tail: something Americans considered a European touch. There was a contrasting roof colour and eventually an elaborate two-tone paint job.

Under the bonnet was Austin's tiny (by US standards) 1.2 L four-cylinder A40 engine. The zero-to-100 km/h sprint was more a stroll. It took around 30 seconds. To market such a small, low-powered, curiously styled vehicle in the US in the 1950s was what *Yes Minister*'s Sir Humphrey Appleby would have called a 'courageous decision'. An increasing number of US cars had twice as many cylinders and four times the engine capacity.

A second wind – okay, gentle breeze – was provided in 1956 by a 1.5 L Metropolitan with revised styling, improved equipment levels and one quarter more power. But sales numbers continued to be modest (to put it politely), and perhaps reached that level only because it was almost impossible to slake America's thirst for new cars in the 1950s.

Within a couple of months of the first Metropolitan going on sale, Nash had merged with Hudson to form American Motors Corporation. So some Hudson-badged Metropolitans were also sold before 1957 when the new concern decided to concentrate on the Rambler brand. At this point the Nash and Hudson nameplates were dropped and the car became simply 'the Metropolitan'. It was also marketed under that simple moniker in the UK when Austin purchased the right to sell it in Blighty. Or, more correctly, the right to fail to sell it in Blighty.

The Metropolitan had set a new direction for American cars, but it was a direction that almost no-one else took. It was finally hit on the head with a brick in 1961, though unsold stock kept showrooms full until well into 1962.

Valiant CM

Corpulent punishment

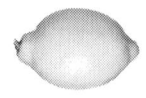

In 1980 there were many exciting things happening on the Australian car market. But none of them involved a dinosaur known as the Valiant.

While Holden turned out its Euro-style Commodore, Ford unveiled the all-new Falcon XD and even small cars were showing previously unimagined performance and refinement, Mitsubishi – yes, Mitsubishi – was building the ancient and lumbering Chrysler Valiant CM.

The CM had been launched by Chrysler Australia in late 1978 and was the final derivative of the VH model of 1971. Rather like those strange creatures that mutate into something entirely different on isolated islands, the final, portly Australian Valiant was a direct descendant of a US 'compact car' that had died out in its homeland.

CM sales brochures boasted 'improved styling features – plus full colour coordination', whatever that meant. But the reality was the 1978 Valiant, with little more than a new grille and taillights, plus various changed body mouldings and badges, was as new as the beleaguered company could manage.

Although it looked bulky, dated and downright boring, and still lacked such basic features as flow-through cabin ventilation, the CM had one thing to commend it: the Electronic Lean Burn System (ELB) on its six-cylinder Hemi engine. Using an early electronic engine management system, Chrysler delivered fuel savings of up to 25 per cent over the previous model.

As well as getting long in the gear-teeth, the Valiant range was shrinking, the main casualty with the CM range being the

Charger coupe, which, for a brief time, had been the company's white knight. Ute and panel van derivatives were also dropped. The base Valiant (which Chrysler called the 'medium-line') gave unrivalled metal for money with a lower price than some small Japanese cars. The Regal was $1700 dearer and the range-topping Regal SE a hopeful $12,002. The top variants were fitted with a 'Fuel Pacer' vacuum device which flashed when the driver was using too much throttle. Oddly, this light was mounted outside the cabin, beneath a chrome shield on the right-hand guard.

In 1979, Chrysler Australia Ltd surprised everyone and made a profit, though this was almost entirely due to sales of Japanese-sourced small cars and didn't ease the overwhelming sense of doom surrounding the company. Chrysler in the States was haemorrhaging and the US corporation sold a third of its Australian operations to Japan's Mitsubishi Corporation for $27 million. In 1980 the rest went for $52 million.

Mitsubishi Australia would have been happy to drop the Valiant but, with 97 per cent of it manufactured down-under, it was needed to meet the company's overall local content targets. Anyway, the tooling was paid for so even a small number could be profitably produced. But while Mitsubishi was happy to keep building the Valiant, it was less enthused about putting its name on it, hence Chrysler badges were retained.

The final blow was the increasing difficulty in finding the small imported parts such as headlight surrounds and wagon tailgate mechanisms. The tiny number of Valiants being produced meant there was no case for making such parts and Chrysler's US warehouses were nearly empty. On 28 August 1981 the last Australian Valiant was driven off the Adelaide assembly line. It was number 565,338, a total little contributed to by the CM, which had sold just 16,005 units in three years.

Toyota T-18

It was launched in December 1979 and heavily promoted as the 'Macho Machine'. Why? Who knows. The T-18 was a listless, flimsy, slightly mis-proportioned hatch with handling on the unfashionable side of ordinary and performance to match.

'Strong gains will be made in the youth market,' skited Toyota, which was claiming as a completely new car a vehicle that was such a parts-bin effort that the steering wheel still bore a 'C' (for Corolla) in its centre rather than a 'T' for whatever T stood for (they never told us).

In specific terms, the T-18 was a four-seater, Japanese-built, three-door hatch with a 'semi-pillarless' side treatment and a sloping rear window. The semi-pillarless design was achieved at the cost of rigidity. *Modern Motor*'s Barry Lake said 'the entire side of the car shakes when the doors are closed with anything more than a gentle touch' and that the T-18 didn't 'stop effectively or safely from any respectable speed'. Even getting up to a respectable speed was a problem as the four-cylinder carburetted engine of this supposedly ultra-masculine powerhouse produced just 54 kW. If you needed a burst of power you were put on a wait-list.

Unsurprisingly, there was no T-19.

Daimler SP250

Strange fish

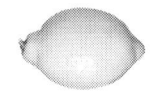

With a heritage dating to the 1890s, the Daimler company had worked hard to shape its reputation as a maker of staid, solid, luxurious conveyances. And it maintained that reputation right up until 1959 when the venerable British company's corporate brain fell out and it decided to release the SP250.

The first and only sports car to wear a Daimler badge wasn't just any old roadster. It was the oddest-looking one in the sports-car world, with bug eyes sticking out of a strangely curved nose and a radiator grille that looked like the mouth of some form of bottom-feeding marine life.

The slab sides were broken up by oddly protruding wheel arches and there was a step in the profile to make way for fins that didn't so much as blend in as blend out. But there was one thing uglier than an SP250 with the top down: an SP250 with its tall, square, ill-fitting canvas roof in the 'up' position.

Aimed squarely at the US market, which was then grabbing every British sports car it could get its hands on, Daimler's roadster was launched as the Dart at the 1959 New York Motor Show. Chrysler had registered 'Dart' and demanded the Daimler name be withdrawn. It could have performed a bigger service for all concerned by demanding the whole car be withdrawn.

'Breathtaking as its performance is Dart's styling!' boasted the original brochure. 'From sleek, fluted grill to flaunting rear fins, every eye-appealing curve of its polyester body expresses the spirit of speed.'

The copy would have served better to deceive if it wasn't placed directly under an illustration of those allegedly eye-appealing curves. Still, the newcomer had disc brakes, which was unusual, and a home-grown V8 engine, which for a British car was even more so. This 2.54 L overhead cam unit was developed from a 'V Twin' Triumph motorcycle engine. Despite this – and the fact it was originally meant to be air-cooled (leading to an under-bonnet spaghetti of cooling hoses on early versions) – the V8 worked surprisingly well and spat out a healthy 105 kW. The problem was the car around it.

The SP250 exhibited atrocious wobbling and shuddering due to a lack of body rigidity. Britain's *Autocar* magazine noted that the driver's door tended to pop open during hard cornering. The omission of bumpers as standard equipment was curious, while handling was average at best and extremely dependent on the right tyre pressures. Top speed, though, was a shade under 200 km/h – an impressive figure helped along by the lightness of the polyester body. Which, presumably, never needed ironing.

As an aside, the reason the English company was called Daimler was because in 1893 Frederick Simms negotiated to build

German Daimler vehicles under licence in Britain. In 1926 the original German company (formed by Gottlieb Daimler) merged with the company started by Karl Benz to become Daimler-Benz. Benz's company had already established the name Mercedes, so the Mercedes-Benz name was used for cars from the merged company. The British firm stuck with Daimler.

For Britain's Daimler, the SP250 ended up not so much an exciting sports adventure as a death throe. In 1960 the company was swallowed by Jaguar. As Jaguar was in the process of preparing its E-Type model for market it had little need for a fish as strange as the SP250. However, orders had been received from American dealers so a decision was taken to proceed with production of the Daimler SP250 and hope for the best.

The best did not eventuate. The US market may have been grabbing every British sports car available, but it was prepared to make an exception in this case.

After about a year, Jaguar engineers heavily reinforced the fibreglass body to stop its scuttle shake. Bumpers became standard equipment. However, the body strengthening didn't stop cracking panels, drooping doors and other problems. What wasn't polyester still had a tendency to rust. And what didn't rust remained unspeakably ugly.

Only 1200 SP250s were sold in left-hand-drive markets, including the US, for whose tastes the styling had supposedly been created. The grand total of all sales, before production officially spluttered to a halt in 1964, was a miserable 2645 units.

Haflinger 700 AP

Little Austrian battler

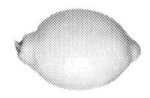

The Steyr-Daimler-Puch Haflinger 700 AP failed to set the Australian market alight, despite its snappy name.

Perhaps the appearance had something to do with it. The vehicle best known as the Haflinger (after a type of mountain pony), or simply the 'Haffie', looked a little like a squashed-nose Mini Moke mounted on stilts.

Imported as a kit, the Haffie was assembled in Melbourne by AFB Bearings from the late 1960s. If the extravagant handle didn't give it away, the radical little beast missed out on being all-Australian by two letters. It was from Graz in Austria.

Claimed as the world's smallest 4WD, the Haflinger had exceptional off-road capabilities that included the ability to climb a 67-per-cent gradient. There was an ingenious chassis layout (rear-mounted engine, independent suspension plus independent front and rear differential locks) and a five-speed gearbox. The diff locks meant the Haffie could keep moving even when only one wheel could find traction, and the provision of portal-style axles (raised above the centre line of the wheels) gave extraordinary ground clearance.

This tiny (643 cc) four-stroke engine developed just 20 kW but considering the Haffie was only about 3.5 metres long, 1.5 metres wide and weighed just 600 kg (less than a third of many of today's four-wheel drives), it pushed the vehicle along adequately. Furthermore, the Haffie could carry almost its own weight as payload. In 1969, *Modern Motor* magazine drove a Haffie to the top of Barrenjoey Head (north of Sydney) 'up the roughest, most precipitous goat track we've ever encountered' and reported 'it would take almost a brick wall to stop it.'

Other press raved too, particularly with the sharp price (around $2190 when the *Modern Motor* article appeared). Yet the public stayed cold. AFB Bearings lost interest too, and assembly passed to Haflinger Sales and Service, then Haflinger Pinzgauer Enterprises.

So why the lack of interest? The Haflinger predated the mainstream vogue for recreational 4WDs by about a decade, and many rural users viewed it with suspicion. It was essentially a military vehicle adapted for private use and, with an air-cooled, horizontally-opposed twin at the rear, it was just a bit too austere and oddball to really take off.

It wasn't a brick wall that eventually stopped the Haffie, it was the new crop of Japanese mini-4WDs that started to appear in the 1970s. Still, 1000 or so Haflingers were assembled in Australia between 1963 and 1976. The last Aussie example was built almost two years after production stopped in Austria.

Edith

As if to prove that not only good things come in small packages, the Australian engineering firm Gray & Harper designed this three-wheeler around 1952.

The Victorian-based company compounded its misdeed three years later by commencing series production. The Edith was claimed as the first micro-car to go into local production and it set new standards for austerity, cartoon styling and misproportioned wheel size. Three brave people could be seated on the Edith's bench seat. A rear-mounted 197 mL Villiers two-stroke engine drove the single rear wheel by chain, cleverly eliminating such frivolities as a drive-shaft, a differential and refinement. The makers claimed the production version would weigh 5 hundredweight and achieve 50 miles per gallon which, when converted into metric, equates to 'terrifyingly light' and 'pretty unimpressive', particularly when you consider a real car such as the Holden could better 30 mpg (9.4 L/100km). Micro-car aficionado Fred Diwell was one of the few to experience an Edith first-hand. His verdict was succinct: 'The very worse car I've had the privilege to ride in.'

Australia's first midget was embraced by no person of any size. The 70-per-year production estimate appears to have peaked at about three or four. If that.

Austin Freeway

Six doesn't sell

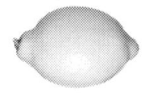

It shared its name with a big road in Texas and had fins just like an American car from the 1950s. But the Austin Freeway of the early 1960s was loudly and proudly advertised as being made by and for Australians. Unfortunately there were more Australians in the 'by' than 'for' category.

The British Motor Company, or BMC, launched the Freeway in 1962 in a dismally misguided attempt to take on Holden, Falcon and Valiant. This attempt was based on the dodgy notion that the success the company had enjoyed with the Mini Minor could be carried up the scale.

Loosely based on the styling of the Austin Farina A60 (and just as loosely built), the Freeway was available in sedan and wagon versions. But whereas the A60 had tried to command a

Holden price with a four-cylinder engine, this was a six – and the Freeway was equipped with features not standard on most other cars of the day, including windscreen washers and a fresh-air heater/demister unit.

An earlier attempt to Australianise a British car, the 1957 Morris Marshall, had featured a thoroughly unconvincing boomerang on the radiator grille. The Freeway didn't win any further points for its tizzy little map of Australia in the centre of its steering wheel.

The reason the Freeway was an Austin was because the latest incarnation of BMC's ever-changing model strategy was to sell its mainstream small cars under the Morris name, family cars as Austins, and luxury vehicles as Wolseleys. Hence a Wolseley version of the Freeway was also built. To help this along, it was given the emotive and instantly memorable name of 24/80. Yes, 24/80.

Like most things to do with the new Austin, the unique, locally built engine was a shortcut, being merely an extended version of the A60's 1.6 L four. Existing factory machinery was used to machine the longer block, saving money. In a similar spirit of making do, the rear fins were taken from Riley and MG sedans (BMC also used these brand-names on a confusing mix of similar cars with different badges and more upmarket detailing). The bonnet was from the A60 but with an extra bit welded to the leading edge and the join hidden behind the favourite decorative device of the day: a chrome strip.

The 2.4 L engine was described as 'the Blue Streak six', which might have been appropriate if oil was blue. Freeway reliability problems included leaks, shrieks and some fairly spectacular engine seizures.

The sales slogan was 'Make way for the Austin Freeway'. Australians did more than that. They gave it the widest berth possible. Precisely 3090 Freeways were sold in the first year, which was also the most successful year. Or least unsuccessful year. To appreciate the size of the failure, consider that the car BMC perceived as the direct competitor, the Holden, sold more examples each and every week than the Freeway had managed in an entire year.

Even fewer Freeways were pushed through the door in year two. In October 1964, a Mark II version was launched, but nobody cared. The name Wolseley disappeared from the market soon afterwards, and Freeway production was discontinued in 1965. Despite this, the company would come back three more times with a local six-cylinder car in the vainglorious hope of taking on the well-entrenched American makes down-under.

AMC Gremlin

Described by its maker as 'the first US designed and built small car which will compete directly with leading imports', this bout of dismay on wheels was essentially the front half of a Rambler Hornet combined with a weird-as-all-get-out chopped tail. This gave the Gremlin all the disadvantages of its larger AMC stablemate, but less interior room.

Designer Richard Teague reputedly sketched the lines of this 1970 offering on the back of an airline sick bag. And as a final brave touch, AMC decided to christen it with a synonym for trouble.

And having decided to build a smaller car how did AMC power it? With the same engines as bigger models. The base donk was a 199 ci, or 3.3 L, six-cylinder while a V8 was optional.

The cheapest version – known as the Commuter – had seats only in the front and sold poorly. The four-seater did slightly better, despite the rear seats being tiny and the occupants often feeling imprisoned behind those huge rear pillars. From a driver's point of view, these pillars created perhaps the biggest blind spot of any American car, while the Gremlin's nose-heavy nature made the handling abominable, particularly with the V8.

The Gremlin was dead in the water by 1978, despite such innovations as 'hockey stick' side stripes, and a Levi's Custom Trim option with seats in nylon meant to look like denim, and punctuated by rivets meant to look like copper. Just before its demise, AMC finally decided to offer a four-cylinder Gremlin. But it was too late, and considering the model's porky weight, it was also too little.

Tatra Electronic

Fancy a spin?

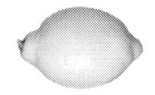

The Tatra T613-4 'Electronic' was displayed at the 1993 Frankfurt Motor Show. The sight produced mixed emotions, though most were happy to see the return to the West of a brand with an exceptionally long and illustrious history.

It was soon after World War I that the eccentric genius Hans Ledwinka built the first of what was to be a long line of Tatra cars. In 1931 the first rear-engined model was seen, and in 1934 the company introduced an air-cooled V8. During that same decade Tatra produced some of the most aerodynamic bodies on the road and built vehicles as varied as a limousine with a 6.0 L V12 and a 528 cc three-wheeler.

When the Western powers so generously gave Czechoslovakia to Hitler just before World War II, the newly installed German officials commandeered local cars – and showed a marked preference for the luxurious Tatras. However, it is said the Germans had so many accidents in these big and eccentric rear-drive Tatras that a general edict was issued prohibiting their use by any member of the occupying forces.

After the war the Marxist government nationalised the plant and insisted the company concentrate on trucks and railway carriages. It would build only as many cars as was necessary to spirit party officials around. But Tatra continued to do things differently. Indeed, it was perhaps the only car-maker in Eastern Europe that remained innovative and interesting throughout the

Communist years, building eccentric rear-engined V8 sedans rather than ancient two-stroke economy cars, or those strange retro-Americana limousines favoured by Politburo members.

It did so, however, with ever-decreasing production numbers.

While the fall of the Berlin Wall suddenly opened huge new markets to companies such as Tatra, it also highlighted the vast gulf between automotive east and west. The Tatra T613-4 seen at the Frankfurt show was sitting among a new crop of Benzes and BMWs that were as modern under the surface as they were above it. In contrast, the Czech machine had a 1960s body hiding mechanical attributes that went back a lot further than that.

The two 1993 models were specially developed for the West, though both were 'fourth generation' variants on the venerable T613 sedan. With a body designed in Italy in 1968 (the first to be styled outside the Tatra factory), this was first produced in 1973. Development cycles in the old Soviet bloc were nothing too speedy or spectacular. In 1980 the first update of the T613, known as the T613-2, introduced black bumpers to replace the chrome ones. Production had peaked in the late 1970s with around 1500 cars produced each year. By the 1980s it was a few hundred. Tatra was only just breathing when the wall came down.

The 'Electronic' variant of the T613-4 – 5 metres long and weighing 1700 kg – was crammed with after-the-fact whizz-bangery, explained in rather tortured prose in the English-language brochures: 'This new class-leading automobile . . . embodies all an up-to-date business-man needs . . . Intelligent self-diagnostic and audiovisual system both speak an eloquent language. This is an ingenious merging of time-tested technology and innovative faculty of Tatra people.'

Power came from an air-cooled, direct injection 3.5 L V8, sitting over the back axle. This engine was probably ready to be dismissed as an antique if not for the impressive 147 kW and 300 Nm output. The mechanical layout, according to the brochure, represented 'the over-rear-axle engined technical conception that guarantees the perfect performance in any road-traffic regime which has, in general, been the privilege of only high-duty sports cars. Both rich-dimensioned energy-absorbing crush zones, resulting in a positive effect onto the all aboard safety are, in the event of an impact, of a great priority.'

Despite the fact the company had once built cars with handling so evil Nazis weren't allowed to drive them, the 1990s model received quite a few complimentary reviews from the German motoring press. Sales, however, stayed in that uncomfortable zone between none and not very many. The story was similar in the UK, where the T613-5 was launched in 1994.

The '5' version – with a cabin heating system that could be programmed up to five days in advance – was to be the last. Just 11 cars were completed in 1996. A revamped version (described as the T700) was displayed in Prague that year but sales did not pick up. The last Tatra car was built in 1998, though plans for a revival have been regularly floated.

Holden HD

Avant guards

Some say it was those sharp protrusions on the front that killed the car off; others insist it was the oddball, slightly effeminate styling, complete with strangely concave rear windscreen and curved sides that emphasised the narrow track.

Whatever the truth, the Holden HD started with a charge when it replaced the hugely successful EH model in February 1965. The HD was wider and slightly longer. However, this was a trick of styling as the increased width was mainly overhang and the extra length (about 50 mm) was largely made up of the pointed guard extensions which would soon cause so much trouble.

Nonetheless, pent-up demand for a new Holden – any new Holden – and a booming economy combined to help the company sell 19,000 HD models during May 1965 alone. After 14 months, nearly 180,000 had been put on the road. Despite this, Holden executives quickly knew they were in trouble. The impressive figures hid a huge public cooling for the HD and an increasing struggle to push each example out the showroom door. By the early months of 1966, Holden's market share had fallen below 40 per cent for the first time since supply of 'Australia's Own' caught up with demand in the early 1950s.

HD highlights included Holden's first disc brakes (though as an extra cost option, and only for the front wheels) and mind-boggling choice of finishes: the steering wheel, for example, was available in 12 colours. Much trumpet-blowing accompanied the launch of Holden's first vinyl roof, available in black or white on the upmarket Premier model. This totally useless Americanism, which served to make the car hotter inside and more prone to rust, was intended to invoke the appearance of a convertible, though with the roof up only.

The new performance engine option, a twin-carb version of the 179 'red motor' introduced with the EH, was known as the X2. Its power was 25 per cent up on standard, making it compare favourably with Ford's 'Super Pursuit' donk. And, even if less torquey than Valiant's 'Slant Six', it avoided having such a silly name.

The HD's auto was no longer the popular Hydramatic but the older, inferior Powerglide, with just two forward speeds. But that wasn't as big a problem for Holden as an American book entitled *Unsafe at Any Speed*. Ralph Nader's landmark 1965 tome pilloried Chevrolet's radical rear-engined Corvair model and made 'road safety' the phrase on everyone's lips. We didn't have Corvairs here but, hey, the Holden was from GM and about the same size. And the HD was the current model.

Soon newspapers were running close-up photos of the HD's front guards and saying these represented a danger to pedestrians. (Never mind the even greater worry caused by the new 'Improved Red Carpet Ride' suspension, which made the HD squirm when asked to change direction.) A media feeding frenzy began. A cynic might suggest that motorists of that era cared no more about pedestrians than today's car buyers (look at those city-bound, bull-barred 4WDs). Nonetheless, most HD buyers were males and found it easier to articulate 'it's unsafe', than 'it looks narrow-tracked and not at all in keeping with the masculine image I require when I spend 36 weeks' pay on a tonne of steel.'

Designers, engineers and production people were pressed to work nights and weekends to hurry the replacement to market by 1966. As well as squaring off the bodywork and cutting back the guard extensions, the replacement HR was graced with a wider track to give it a more stable stance. Later it was joked that HD stood for 'Horribly Designed' and HR for 'Hastily Rectified'.

Standard Vanguard

The first Standard Vanguard represented a bold attempt to give a small postwar British car some US design razzamatazz. Bolder still, Standard's accountants demanded it be achieved without the cost of sending anyone to America. Head stylist Walter Belgrove was apparently despatched with his sketchbook to the US Embassy in London in the hope he could sight some American iron being driven in or out. The resulting Vanguard was launched in July 1947.

That US lines didn't quite work on a short British chassis is hardly a surprise. There was another problem. The word 'standard' was once primarily considered in terms of the phrase: 'Setting the . . .'. However, with widespread use of names such as Deluxe, it came to mean 'pretty damn ordinary'. Which in this case was spot-on.

In 1961 Standard became a division of Leyland Motors, an English expression meaning doomed. Within three years it was a dropped Standard.

Bristol Blenheim

Old bomber

You may be able to forgive a four-speed gearbox, solid rear axle, pushrod engine, separate chassis and general dearth of modern technology in a 21st-century car if it is extremely cheap or looks drop-dead gorgeous. But what about when it costs a motza and looks like a 1970s Ford Capri coupe suffering from water retention?

That's the question one has to ask with the Bristol Blenheim, a conveyance still in production in the noughties and priced as we go to press at something exceeding £140,000. Yes, do not adjust your book. That price was £140,000, or nearly $350,000.

The Blenheim shares its names with the city in which it is built and a World War II fighter-bomber from the days when Bristol was a major aviation manufacturer. Which was a very long time ago. After World War II, with something of a slump in aircraft demand, Bristol took the same route as Messerschmitt and others: it turned to cars. To ease the transformation, Bristol bought licences from BMW and produced its own versions of these German cars in the UK.

Bristol Cars had some success at Le Mans in the early 1950s and, since the very early 1960s, the brand has been in the hands of a former racing car driver named Tony Crook. The 1960s and 1970s brought a series of Chrysler-engined cars, some taking aviation-themed names such as Beaufighter and Brigand. The Blenheim coupe's flat-sided, oddly proportioned shape goes back to the 603 model of the mid-1970s, though it seems the name Blenheim wasn't used until the 1990s.

The official production estimate for the Blenheim is 'no more than 150 per year', though an independent estimate puts it perhaps more realistically at 'around two'. No outsiders are allowed to visit the factory where the cars are banged together – sorry, hand-crafted – because the workers are supposedly also involved in secret design work for the aviation industry. Which hopefully is a little more up to date than anything they are doing with road vehicles.

But back to the appearance of the Blenheim car. The official literature avoids terms such as 'porky piece of 1970s excess', preferring the more reassuring affirmation that the appearance 'is carefully tailored to achieve quiet understatement yet maintain an elegant, timeless line'. It also says the Blenheim – the product, it adds, of the only luxury car-maker under British control – takes three to four times as much labour to build as other luxury cars and is a 'true gentleman's Grand Touring coupe . . . favoured by the most skilled and enthusiastic drivers'.

'In a Bristol,' we are told, 'every journey becomes an occasion, a relaxing and satisfying place from which to observe the hectic world without.'

Inside are the usual British luxury accoutrements, including soft leather seats, thick carpets and slabs of walnut veneer, though assembled with 1960s and 1970s construction techniques and design sensibilities. To save cost the Blenheim incorporates many off-the shelf components such as Vauxhall rear light clusters, while beneath that 1970s body is pure 1950s technology. There's a huge separate chassis under a hand-beaten aluminium skin. This soft and expensive aluminium doesn't result in particularly light weight, though. The Blenheim weighs nearly 1.8 tonnes despite being a comparatively modest 4.87 metres long.

The engine, a 5.9 L V8 borrowed from Chrysler, is also ye olde worlde. A four-speed auto box is standard, and a bi-fuel engine (petrol and LPG) was offered circa 2003 to reduce running costs and improve emissions.

Electronics? Not many. Bristol claims its own mechanical brake assist system, for example, gets along very well without the need for any nancy-pantsy computer-controlled antilock overrides. A stability control system? Yeah, sure. It's called the steering wheel.

The claimed performance is rest-to-100 km/h in a spritely 6.3 seconds, but this and claims of outstanding aerodynamics, leading refinement and stunning performance have been hard to verify, since members of the press are not given access to evaluation vehicles. Well, they might give away secrets to Jerry, old boy.

Alfa Romeo Montreal

Neurotic exotic

As the 1960s turned into the 1970s, Alfa Romeo was a company in crisis. So nothing out of the ordinary there.

On this occasion the confusion and upheaval were due to a surprise decision to build an entirely new high-volume small car (the Alfasud) in an entirely new factory in Naples, rather than the traditional home of Alfa, Milan. This precipitated a bizarre form of warfare, characterised by misinformation and even sabotage, between Alfa workers in the north and south.

And if that wasn't enough, amid the rushed and fraught development of what was to be its smallest, cheapest car, the company decided to simultaneously develop the most expensive and complicated car in its history. On mature reflection, it might have been just a bit too much.

The newcomer was based on a Bertone-designed coupe presented at Expo '67 in Montreal (hence the un-Italian name), though the official announcement of the production version didn't come until March 1970 and it would be another year before any production examples rolled off the end of the line.

That the Montreal looked the part was never a point of argument. It also introduced Alfa Romeo's first ever V8 engine for the street (pre-war Alfa eights had an inline configuration), in the form of a downsized version of the company's famous 3.0 L racing engine. This was an all-alloy, 2.6 L, quad cam, 16-valve, dry-sumped donk with mechanical fuel-injection. If nothing else, it was a triumph of compactness. Most Italian car makers needed 12 cylinders to fit in as much complexity and temperamental character as Alfa had managed with eight.

This new engine drove through a five-speed ZF manual floor shift. Or didn't, if the mood took it.

One of six Montreal prototypes was flown to Australia for a promotional tour. *Wheels* magazine published a rave road test in its July 1971 issue, and relayed the official promise that right-hand drive production models would be available shortly. The word 'shortly' means different things to different people. Although many local Alfaholics quickly signed up for Montreals, it would be three long years before Australian-spec 'right hookers' were available.

If considered a fully-fledged Italian supercar, the Montreal was well priced at around $15,000. That made it a Porsche 911S competitor in cost, yet its performance statistics were closer to the much dearer Ferrari Dino and Lamborghini Urraco.

The Montreal had exotic features such as power-assisted ventilated discs front and rear. But, boy, every foible of Alfa ergonomics was there in abundance, with poor vision, lousy ventilation, a driving position that could be adjusted between uncomfortable and very uncomfortable, and a dated dashboard with a layout which defied any normal conventions of utility. Reliability and durability were, alas, everything you'd expect (indeed there are some of us who maintain that at Alfa Romeo the CEO reports to the spare parts manager). And then there was the battle the owners had yet to fight: with rust.

The Montreal would be sold in Australia for only two years. Of a total production run of almost 4000, just 200 were built in right-hand drive.

Amphicar

This product of German and British engineering cleverly combined the drawbacks of a car with the drawbacks of a boat.

Launched – literally – during the late 1950s, the Amphicar was one of the most successful amphibian road cars ever made, which is a very generous way of saying a few were sold before the company went broke.

The Amphicar used Triumph Herald mechanical components, an adventurous starting point considering these same components struggled in the comparatively lightweight Herald. And the Amphicar's road manners were everything you'd expect of a heavy vehicle with a high centre of gravity that combined the wheelbase of a Mini Minor with the overall length of a family sedan.

The four-seater convertible was driven by its rear wheels on land and by twin propellers in the water. That water needed to be very still for the Amphicar to reach the claimed top water speed of 8 km/h. In rough water it could go backwards. And there was no rudder – the front wheels were meant to make it change direction, something they didn't always want to do.

Another problem was complying with conflicting marine and road legislation: the company was dangerously close to having a vehicle that could only be used in international waters. And it was a very brave person who was prepared to lose sight of land in an Amphicar.

It was said that at least six Amphicars came to Australia during the mid-1960s. In 1968 the whole project sank.

Isuzu Minx PH10

Bad to worse

In the early 1950s the Japanese deserved their reputation as makers of rotten little cars with little to commend them. After all, they were mostly building British and French automobiles that perfectly matched that description.

Not only that, the emerging Japanese car-makers were doing it with low technology (even by the standards of the cash-strapped postwar European industry), and in undercapitalised factories which often had dirt floors and were staffed by strike-prone employees with little or no experience in the motor industry.

Soon after World War II, Japan's all-powerful industrial body, MITI, had demanded an indigenous motor industry. To this end it produced legislation which would effectively end the importing of cars from 1952. However, MITI knew local car-makers had to do an apprenticeship, so suggested they start assembling the latest small Euro cars (more suitable for Japanese roads than US cars, and cheaper), while a components industry was developed that would allow full local manufacture.

The result was such curio-atrocities as the Isuzu version of the Hillman Minx and an equally loathsome series of Datsun-built Austins from Nissan. During the same period, a string of horrendously ugly and unstable locally conceived passenger cars also appeared.

Anglo-autophilia was nothing new in Japan. In 1918, a corporate ancestor of Isuzu signed a deal to produce Wolseley cars. Nissan built a version of the Austin 7 in Japan before the war, and produced the A40 under an official agreement with Austin from 1952.

Nissan was dogged by strikes and several times it tottered on the edge of bankruptcy. Yet through most of the 1950s, Nissan-Austins were the best-selling cars in Japan, with the company's production topping 20,000 for the first time in 1957.

Hino (the bankrupt carcass of which would later be absorbed into Toyota) opted to produce Renaults. As built in Japan between 1953 and 1961, these rear-engined French machines quickly gained a reputation for breaking up on country roads. In the same year that Hino took the Gallic route, Isuzu struck its deal with The Rootes Group to produce Hillmans. Isuzu had produced a few cars before and after World War II, but commercial vehicles had mostly been the mainstay of the company.

The 1953 Isuzu Minx PH10 model had a 1.4 L side-valve engine developing 43 bhp (around 32 kW) at 4400 rpm. By 1957 the Minx was entirely manufactured in Japan, though its sales lagged well behind that of Nissan's Austins.

When rendered with the Japanese technology of the 1950s, the Minx was even heavier, slower and less refined than the original. Similarly, Nissan's Austins gave little hint that we would soon see an automotive juggernaut in the East, a country producing cars so well-finished and well-equipped they would force European and American manufacturers to completely reassess the way they designed, built and marketed their cars.

For all their faults, there was a pay-off with those early Japanese copy-cars: although they were crude and heavy, most were also rugged. This was thanks partly to over-engineering and, as the 1950s progressed, to improvements made to the original designs by fast-learning Japanese engineers. When two Austin-based Datsun Bluebird 1000s were sent to compete in the 1958 Mobilgas Around-Australia Trial, they showed themselves better able to handle rough Australian roads than the original donor cars. One scored a class win. Yes, it was in a class with little competition, but the feat caused huge pride in Japan.

From there things moved quickly. In 1959 Nissan produced its first truly home-grown Bluebird and in 1961 Isuzu produced the Bellel. It was a four-door sedan that looked remarkably like an Austin but was claimed as an original production. Greater success came for Isuzu with the Bellett of 1963, by which time the Japanese were less interested in praising British cars than burying them. It is a mission now pretty well complete.

Trabant P601

Worker's Triumph

The widely held belief that the bodywork of the East German Trabant was reinforced with cardboard was a vicious lie spread by anti-revolutionary forces in the pay of capitalist roaders.

There was no cardboard in the body of the glorious people's car of the German Democratic Republic. To strengthen its Duraplast outer panels, the Trabant used nothing less than genuine cotton fibre.

The Trabi – as it became commonly known – was much more than a car. It was a subject of derision, an environmental disaster, a danger to those inside and out and an international declaration that Communism didn't work.

Ironically, the eastern parts of Germany had a fine tradition of car building. Before World War II, the Horch luxury brand, which was part of the Auto Union concern, was produced in the same Zwickau factories that later disgorged the Trabant. But unfortunately when the East German workers seized control of the means of production from their exploiters after the war, automotive standards quickly slipped behind those of the running dog capitalists on the other side of the divide.

The Trabi was the product of the Sachsenring company, which, after producing tractors and trucks during the late 1940s, turned to making cars based on pre-war designs from the DKW company. These had front-mounted two-stroke engines and – by the mid-1950s – bodywork made from Duraplast. This cotton fibre-reinforced resin was cheaper and easier to come by than steel (which the military had first call on, anyway). And, unlike fibreglass, it could be shaped in a press and didn't need to be painted, as long as you were happy with a finish like a Bakelite radio.

Sachsenring's P70 model – unveiled amid government-approved levels of excitement at the 1955 Leipzig Fair – captured the essential ingredients of the later Trabant; indeed a slightly smaller version produced from 1957 (the P50) was the first vehicle to use the Trabant name.

The Trabant P50 was car-making at its most basic but could transport four adults in discomfort. It mutated into the P60, then in 1964 a major reskinning produced the longest-running and best-known Trabant, the P601.

The Trabant P601 was not a complete disaster from day one. There were economy cars on the other side of the divide that were very similar: the Goggomobil sedan, for example. But the likes of Goggomobil knew when to stop, which was very quickly. The Trabi P601, however, kept going for nearly 30 years and became internationally infamous when thousands of them noisily spluttered through the ruins of the Berlin Wall in 1989.

The P601 was powered by a 600 cc two-stroke twin, which was air-cooled for lower cost and higher noise. And the bodywork looked like a child's drawing of a Triumph Herald, itself several years old in 1984 and no oil painting.

The Trabi P601 had a big door on each side that never looked properly closed, and silly little fins on the tail, even with the station wagon version. But what was it like to drive? Crap, actually. It was noisy, smoky, smelly and badly built, with shocking brakes, dire performance, miserable handling and a 6-volt electrical system so dismal you almost needed a torch to see if the headlights were on.

However, improvements were made in ensuing years, transforming the Trabi from a primitive, badly built Eastern European deathtrap into a primitive, badly built Eastern European deathtrap with a 12-volt electrical system.

With the glasnost and perestroika of the late 1980s, an agreement was reached for VW to supply 1.1 L four-stroke Polo engines for an improved 1988 version of the P601. When Communism collapsed soon afterwards, the two-stroke was phased out completely and only Polo-engined models were built. Not that anyone much wanted them; with no restrictions on what cars they bought, people from the East could finally turn their backs on Duraplast and tailfins.

Despite the odiousness of the styling, mechanical attributes and build quality, Trabants were exported in small numbers to even non-Communist countries from the 1960s. In the 1990s the car became positively trendy as a symbol of the old East. Working and non-working examples turned up as everything from highly decorated weekend runabouts to components of conceptual artworks. Production finally stopped in 1991.

Ford Falcon XK

The weakest links

No-one could deny it was a more modern-looking car than the FB Holden. It was more sophisticated too. Just look at its low-slung body, its 'space-age' concave grille, its more powerful engine, its optional automatic transmission.

Yes, next to the boxy Holden, the brand new Australian-built Falcon of 1960 looked like a clear winner. There was only one small problem . . .

Before we come to that, here's the background. Ford Australia had been trying to take on Holden with the British-sourced (but locally assembled) Zephyr, and it just wasn't working. The Zephyr was markedly dearer than the Holden and its design was such that even full local manufacture would not enable Ford bean counters to get sufficient cost out of it. And, let's face it, the name was stupid.

By 1957, Ford Australia's market share was a dismal 13.7 per cent. The solution appeared to lie in the US where the Big Three were preparing 'compact cars' for 1959 to counter the success of such imports as the VW Beetle. Ford Australia decided to extend its Victorian facilities and manufacture the new US Falcon, which was not only more svelte than the Zephyr but lighter and cheaper to build.

With the aim of achieving 95 per cent local content from the outset, Ford Australia spent a then-huge $30 million in the lead-up to the Falcon launch. Trouble was, remarkably little of that money was spent on local testing. The triple claim that 'Falcon is Australian . . . built entirely in Australia, for Australian conditions' equated to a lie, a damned lie and a bald-faced whopper.

Codenamed XK, the first Aussie Falcon was powered by Ford Australia's first locally manufactured donk: a 2.4 L, six-cylinder OHV engine developing 67 kW at 4200 rpm. This was linked to a three-speed manual gearbox or a two-speed 'Fordomatic' auto.

Early sales figures seemed to support the optimism of the marketing men. By 1961 Ford Australia's market share had risen to 19.4 per cent. But by then Falcon engineers and many customers had already realised that what worked on the smooth roads of the US of A proved a lot less successful down-under. Front suspension ball joints, particularly, were failing to withstand the worst suburban roads, let alone the outback.

Running changes tended to expose other weaknesses. The irony was that Ford had inadvertently added substance to Holden's parochial 'built for Australian conditions' mantra. Indeed, the new Falcon actually helped along the sales of that dated piece of 1950s kitsch that was Holden's FB/EK series.

As Ford Australia's management battled increasing warranty claims, falling sales and the 'foul can' nickname, its engineers vigorously set about the task of product improvement. No amount of vigour was worth anything, of course, if the money wasn't there. And for a while it was touch-and-go whether the Australian Falcon would make it through. Eventually the US agreed to underwrite the huge cost of rectifying the cars already sold and the further expense of developing local, tougher parts.

By 1962 the sales slump had been effectively arrested and the image was improving. In that year the revised XL model, with its enduring slogan of 'Trim, Taut and Terrific', was launched and a

Falcon was driven to victory in the most important local production car race of 1962, the Armstrong 500 at Phillip Island. The Australian Falcon had been finally rescued from Lemondom, but by then GM had responded with a Holden at least as modern-looking as the Falcon, and a golden opportunity was lost.

Toyota Publica 700

In the early 1960s enough Australians thought they'd look good in a cheap Tiara to encourage Toyota to launch the even smaller Publica 700.

The Publica – the name perhaps deriving from the Latin for 'flimsy and odious' – was a finned, two-door sedan with styling that pre-empted that of the Trabant, a vehicle with styling that did not need pre-empting.

Billed as 'Australia's cheapest car', the Publica was also among its noisiest, slowest and hardest to like. Even back then some windscreen wiper motors had more kick than the Publica's 700 cc twin-cylinder air-cooled screecher, arguably the worst single piece of mechanical equipment to come out of Japan's largest car-maker.

Trying to keep up with the traffic was a problem because, by the time the Publica had built up a decent head of steam, most of the traffic had already arrived where it was going. When fitted with the optional two-speed automatic transmission, the Publica took 53 seconds to accelerate from rest to 100 km/h. A modern family sedan takes about 8 seconds.

However, Toyota's adventure with miniature cars was almost over. In 1966 the company assumed a controlling interesting in Daihatsu and delegated to that company the job of producing tiny, underpowered, screaming little horrors.

Davis

The boot scooter

It looked like a full-size dodgem car. Or perhaps a shoe. It had three wheels and, although claimed as a four-seater, all the passengers were placed in a straight line across one padded bench.

It was to be built by an entirely new company in California (not exactly the heart of the US motor industry) and powered by a Hercules engine normally used for stationary applications, such as roving military spotlights. Stability was questionable, and a weird quirk of the suspension system meant the nose actually rose during heavy braking.

But there was madness in the methods. And fraud too. Behind the claimed 'world's biggest three-wheeler' was one Gary Davis, born in Indiana in 1904. During the 1920s and 1930s Davis worked as a used car salesman while building an impressive collection of ex-wives, creditors and disgruntled business partners. Shortly after World War II, Davis decided to build his own car.

One of Davis's claims was that legendary screen actress Greta Garbo was among his financiers. If a lie, it was an ingenious one, as silent partners wouldn't have come much more silent than Garbo. As for the car itself, the origins appear to lie with motor racing engineer Frank Kurtis, who built a three-wheel roadster with a V8 engine circa 1940. This provided a complete departure from the usual idea that a three-wheeled layout was the domain of underpowered economy cars.

After a scam that enabled Gary Davis to acquire Kurtis's three-wheeler for $50, the vehicle was modified and rebadged. Davis's head engineer, Peter Westburg, later described his boss as a 'quick talker with a ready grin that made you feel at ease . . . He could borrow the shirt off your back and sell it back to you and you would swear that you had gotten a bargain.'

The unveiling of the oddly curved aluminium-bodied Davis car – to sell for a bargain basement $995 – came with huge razzle dazzle. In a series of road-shows across the United States in 1947 and 1948, the public was transfixed by such innovations (or gimmicks) as hidden headlights and built-in hydraulic jacks that could raise the body automatically when a tyre needed changing. Indeed, in some places the Davis created almost as much excitement as the bigger, flasher Tucker of the same era.

When people questioned the stability of such a large three-wheeler, Davis paid a Hollywood stunt driver to attempt to turn the car over, apparently without success. Celebrities, including actor Red Skelton, were drafted into the promotional effort and commission agents, it seems, were taking orders with deposits almost as soon as the prototype was displayed. Hundreds of people also signed on as dealers, raising as much as $1.2 million.

The Davis was a grab-bag of borrowed parts. Many things changed from one car to the next; one early prototype seems to have had a V8 (as with the car it was based on), another a six, but most were powered by the front-mounted four-cylinder Hercules, which drove the rear wheels. No matter which engine was fitted, however, Davis's claim of '100 mph and 50 mpg' was nonsense of the utter variety.

Many people believe Preston Tucker, for all his shortcomings, intended to build and sell his controversial Tucker 48. Fewer believe Davis had any such plans for his car. There was plenty of money coming in but little evidence it was being spent on the things needed to meet the proposed production schedule of 50 cars per day in 1947, ramping up to 100-a-day in 1948.

The things Davis did spend company money on, according to court records, included a Beverly Hills home for himself, mink coats for acquaintances and various other items not entirely necessary for volume automotive production. And by one account none of Davis's workers ever received a pay cheque for their efforts.

While those who had purchased dealer franchises were screaming for cars that never seemed to arrive, legal authorities were trying to unravel the highly creative corporate structure that had been created. They succeeded and, with just 17 Davis cars built, the man with his name on the bodywork was hauled off to jail for fraud and the car-making operation wound up. Davis was released after two years and died in 1973.

Index of Cars

Alfa Romeo Montreal, 144
AMC Pacer, 73
AMC Gremlin, 131
Amphicar, 147
Austin Freeway, 128
Austin X6, 18

Bond Bug, 21
Bristol Blenheim, 140

Chevrolet Corvair, 6
Chrysler Centura, 66

Daihatsu Bee, 99
Daimler SP250, 120
Datsun 280ZX, 30
Davis, 160

Edith, 127

Fiat ESV 1500, 25
Fiat Croma, 14
Ford Cortina Six, 22
Ford Falcon EA, 54
Ford Falcon XK, 156
Ford Gyron, 95
Ford Landau, 78
Ford Pinto, 108

Haflinger 700 AP, 124
Hillman Imp, 34
Holden Brougham, 100
Holden Camira, 70
Holden HD, 136
Holden Piazza, 46
Honda Z, 42

Ilinga AF2, 96
Isuzu Minx PH10, 148

Jaguar XJ220, 1
Jensen Interceptor, 62

Lada 110, 33
Leyland Force 7, 65
Lightburn Zeta Sports, 10
Ligier, 57

Moller Skycar, 41
Moskvich, 103

Nash Metropolitan, 112
Nissan Cedric, 5

Oldsmobile Toronado, 50

Panther 6, 82

Panther Rio, 77
Prenvic, 4
Purvis Eureka, 74

Quasar, 17

Sabra Sports, 89
Scamp, 49
Ssangyong Korando, 85
Standard Vanguard, 139
Subaru 360, 26
Suzuki X90, 86

Tatra Electronic, 132
Toyota 2000GT, 104
Toyota Corona 'Starfire', 38
Toyota Publica 700, 159
Toyota T-18, 119
Trabant P601, 152
Triumph Mayflower, 69
Tucker 48, 90

Valiant CM, 116
VW Country Buggy, 58

Zil, 45